Beautiful Inverted Nature
Arya Bàhram

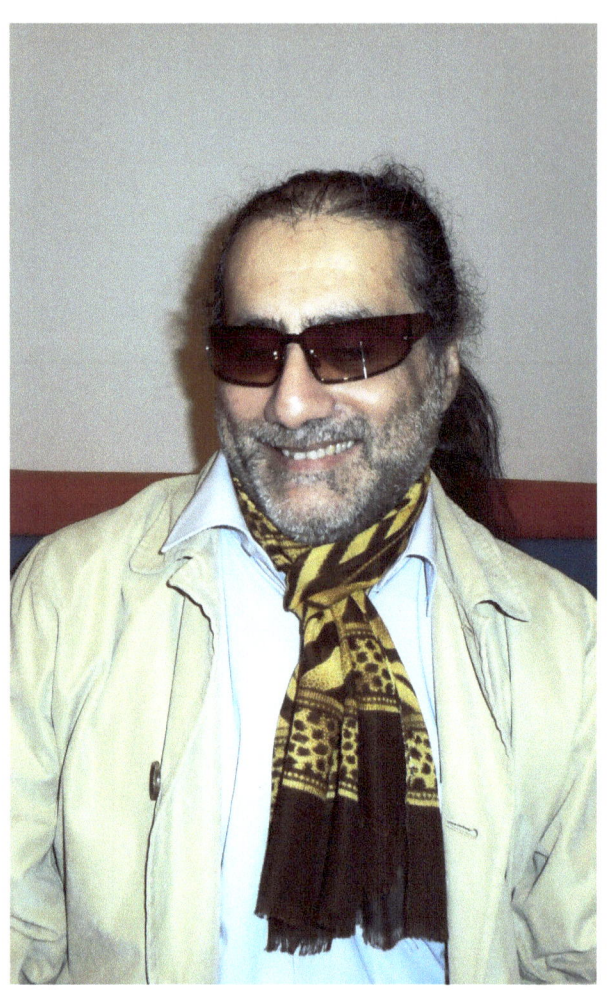

Beautiful Inverted Nature
Arya Bàhram

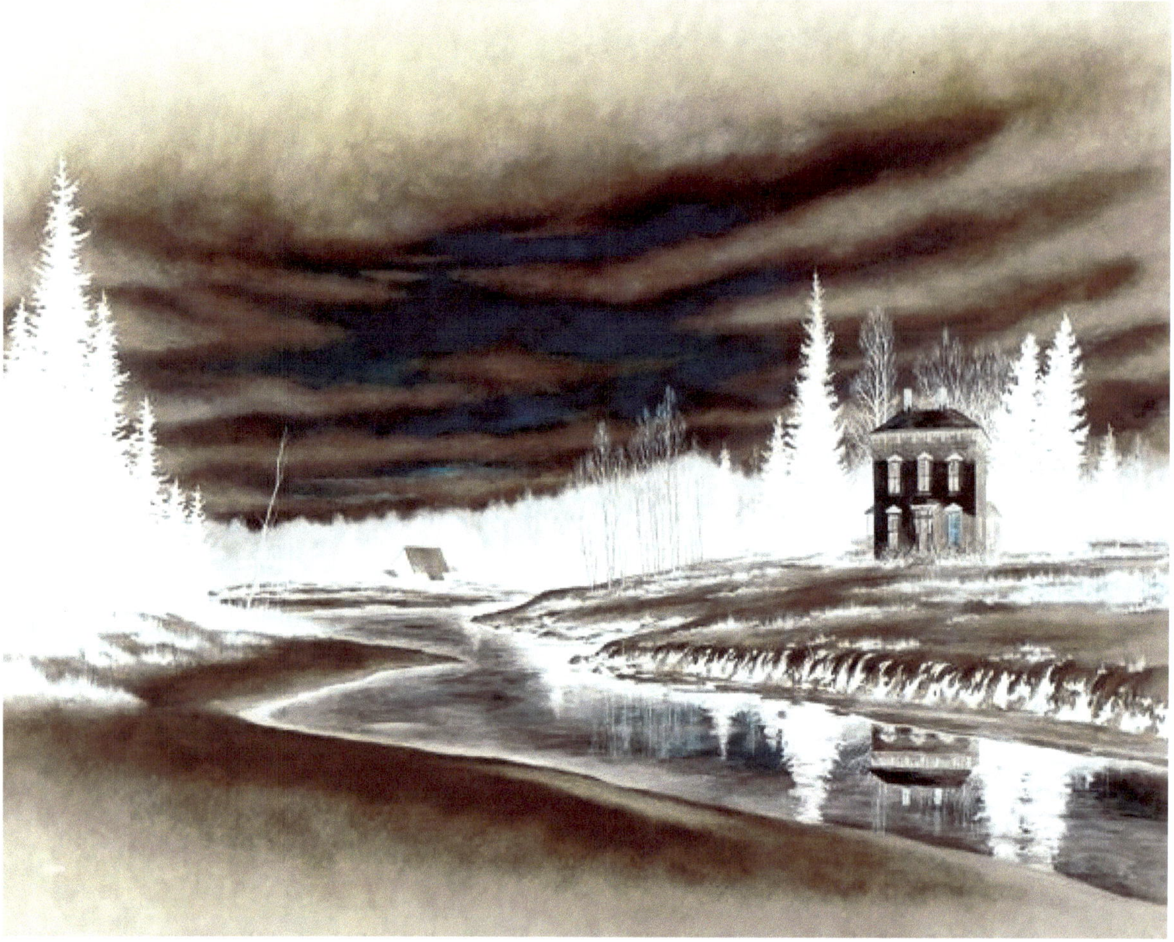

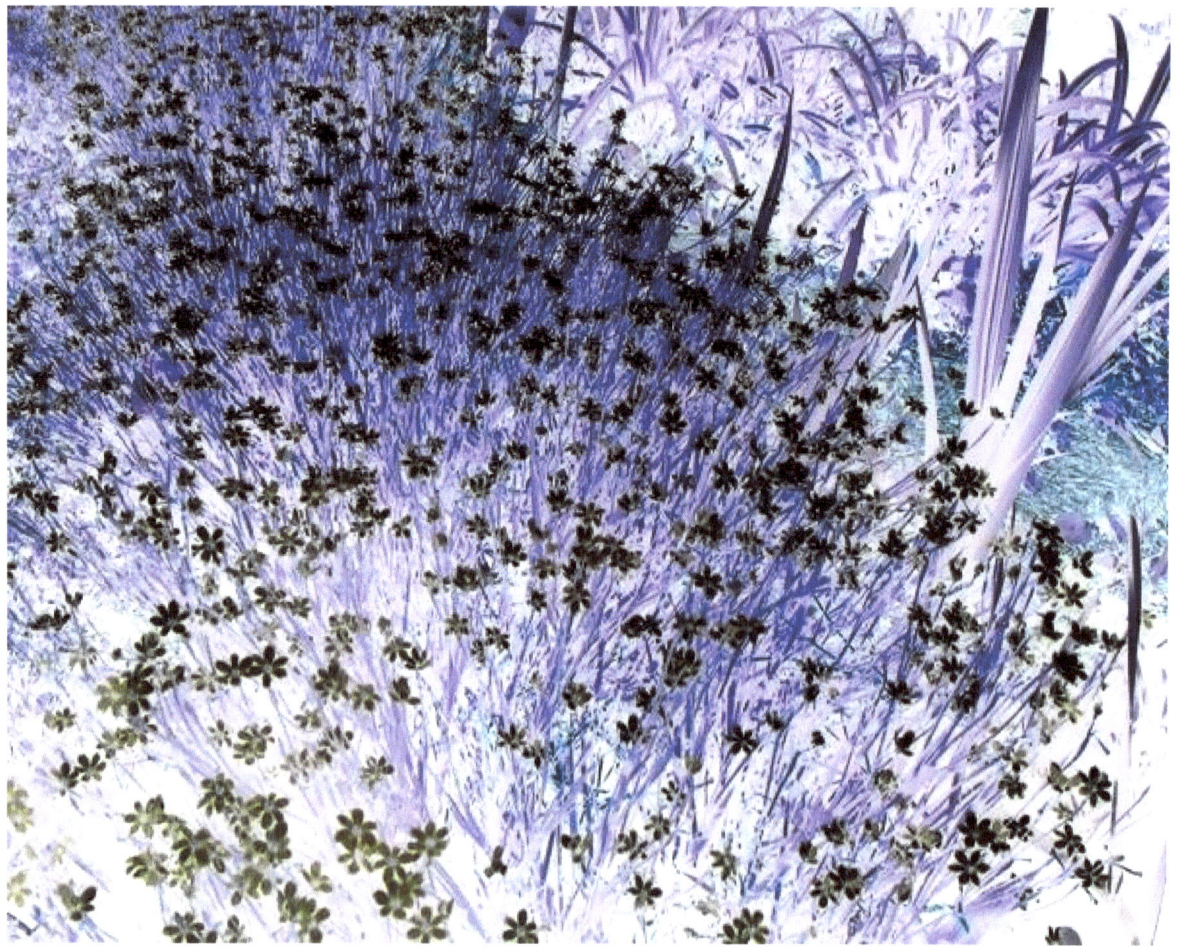

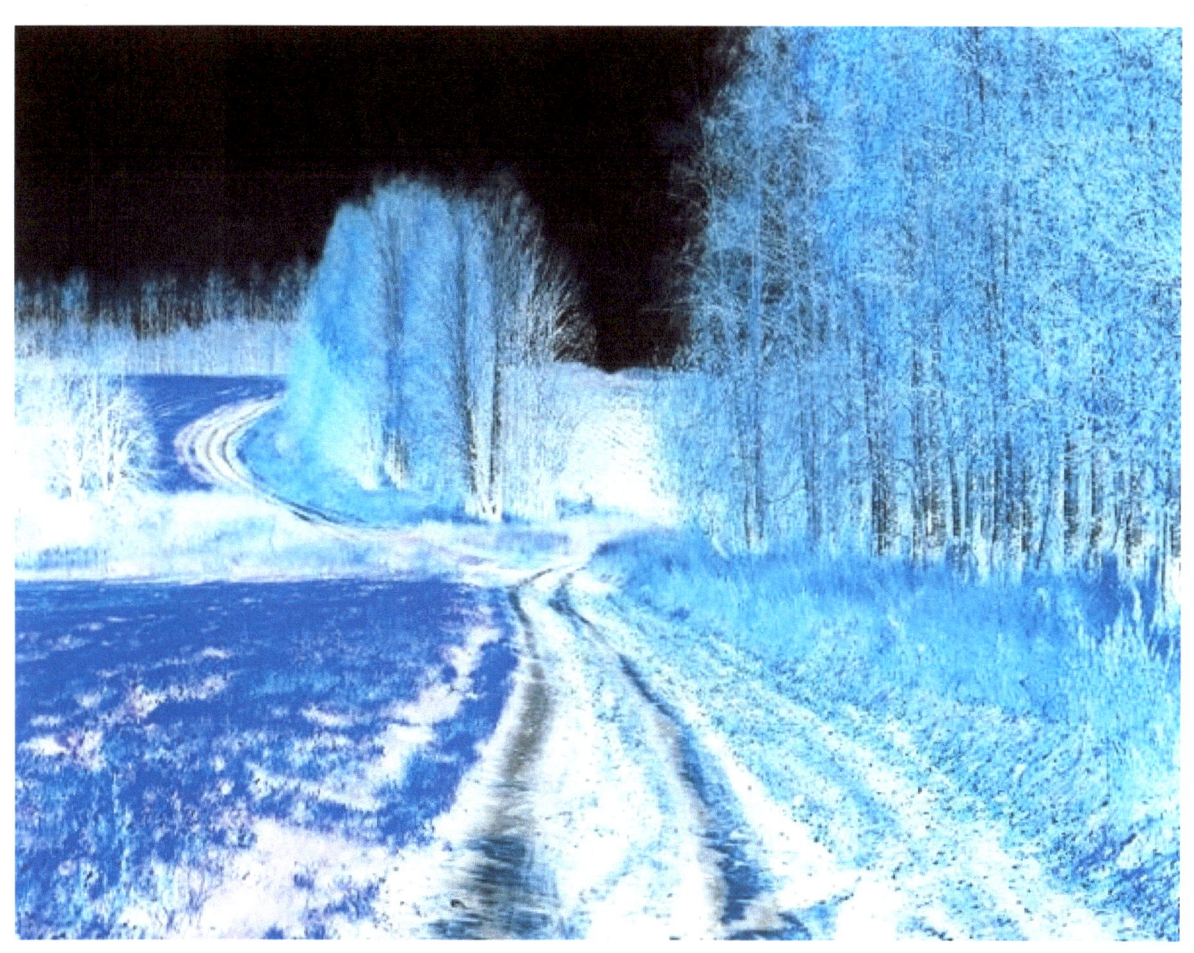
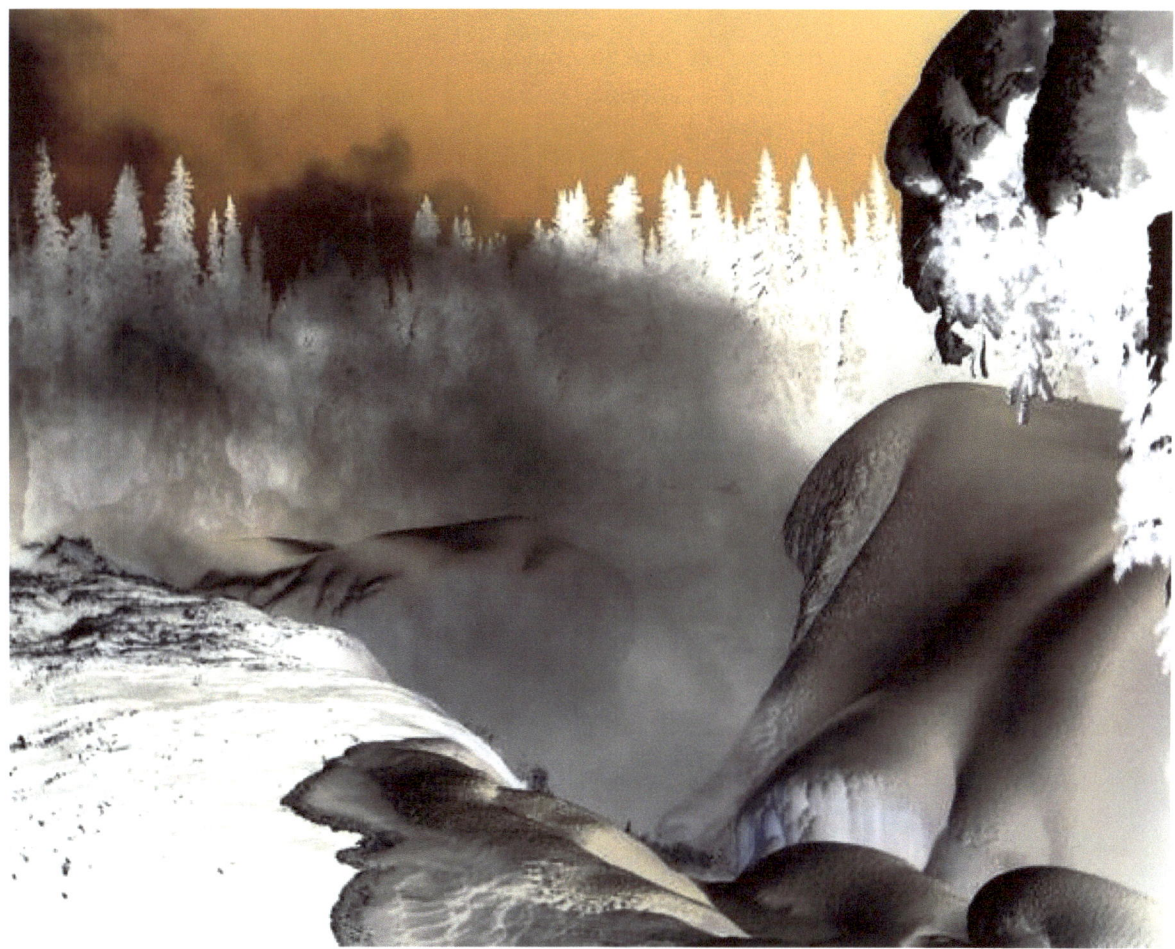

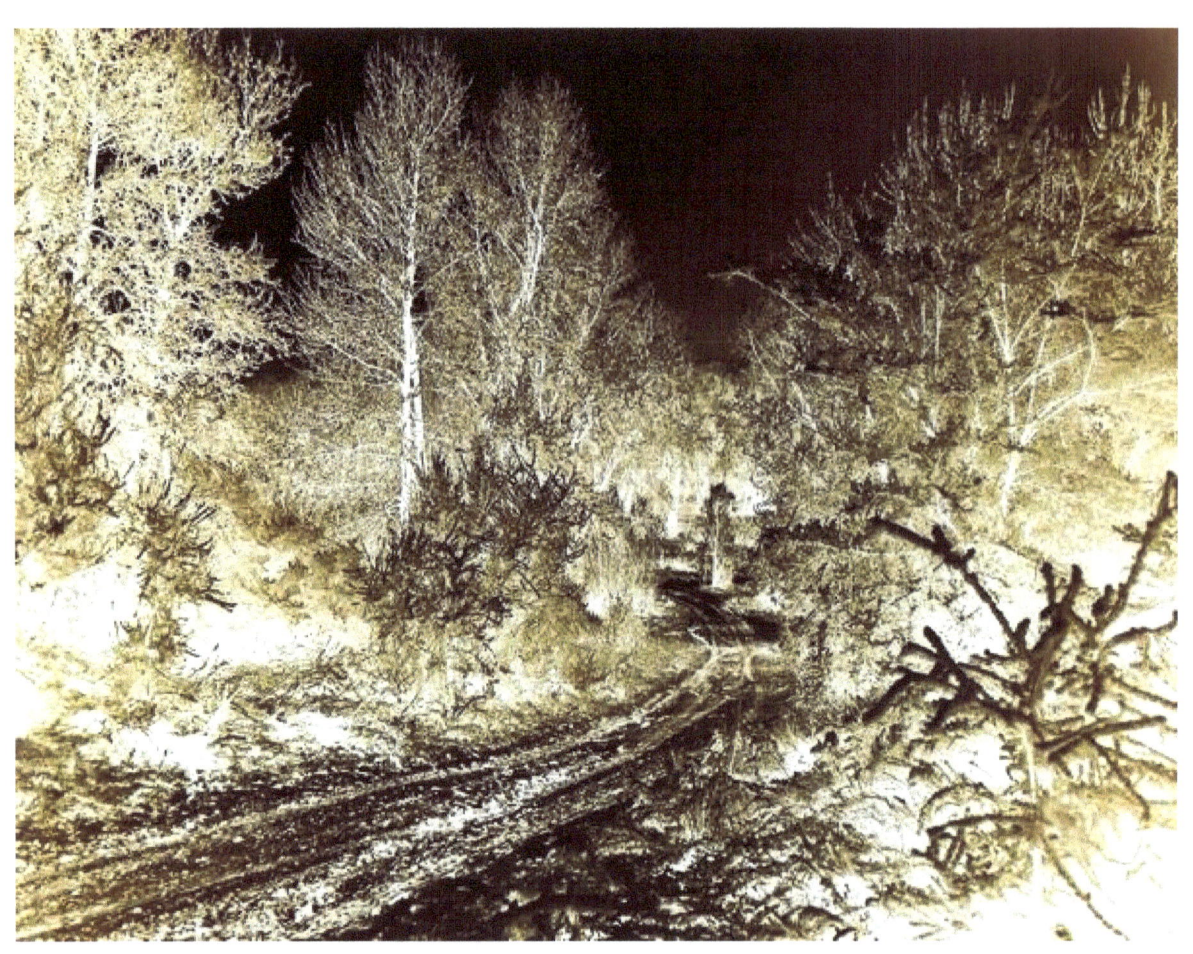
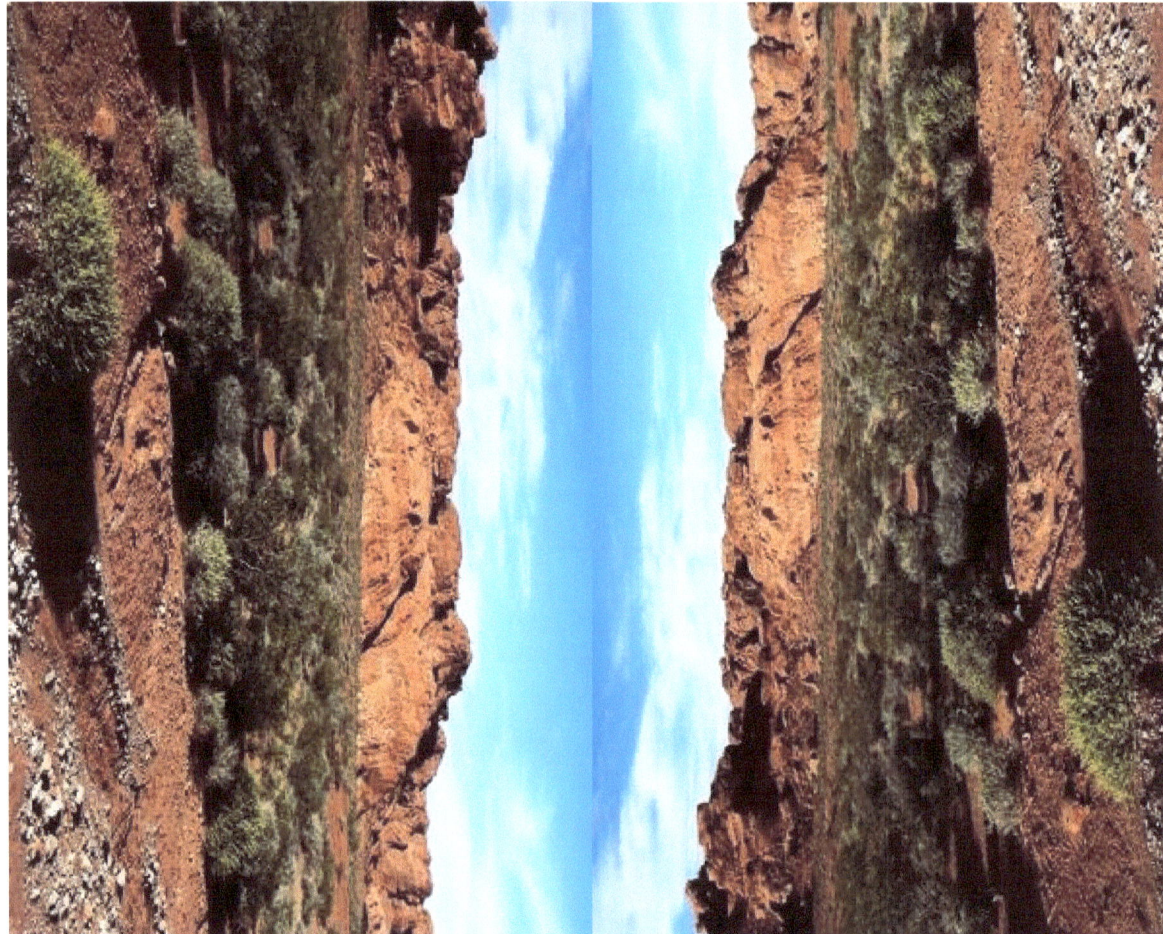

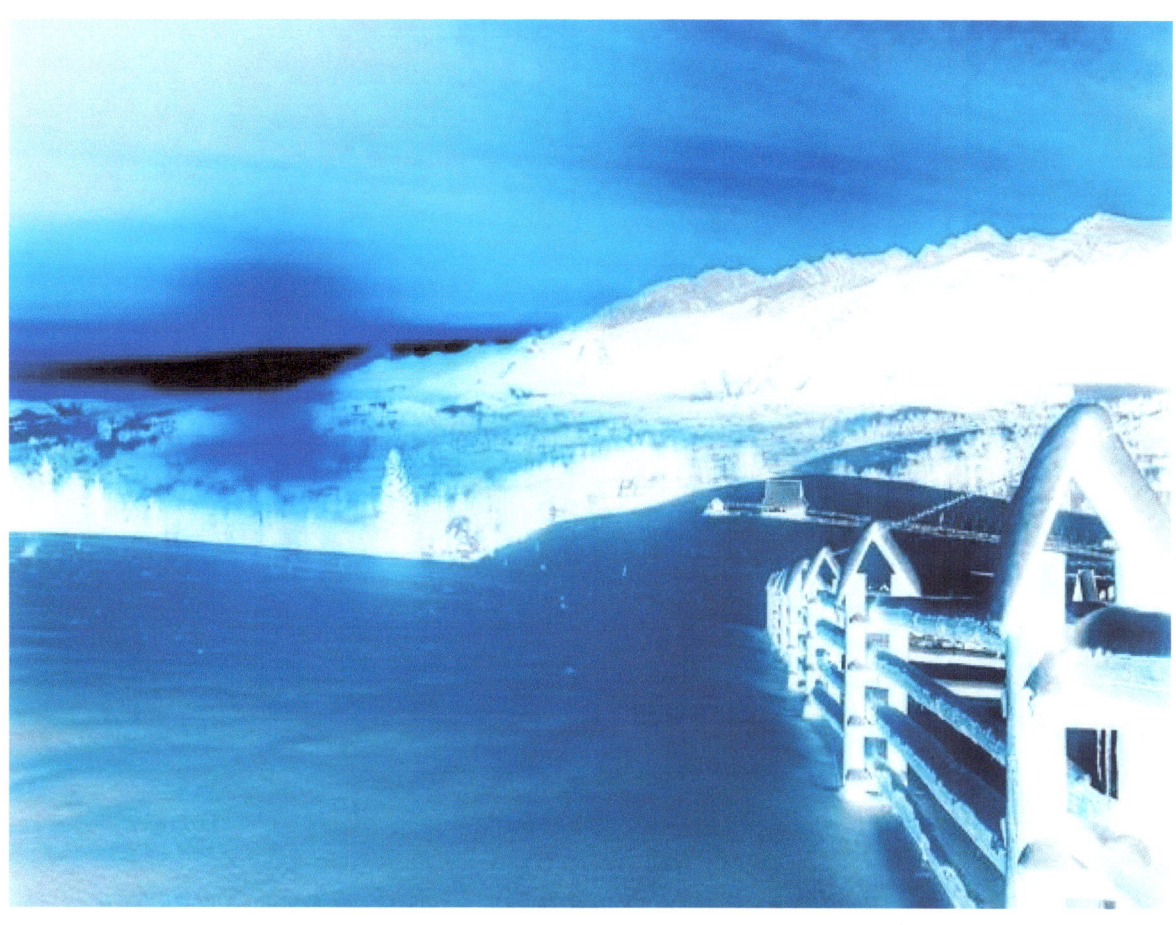

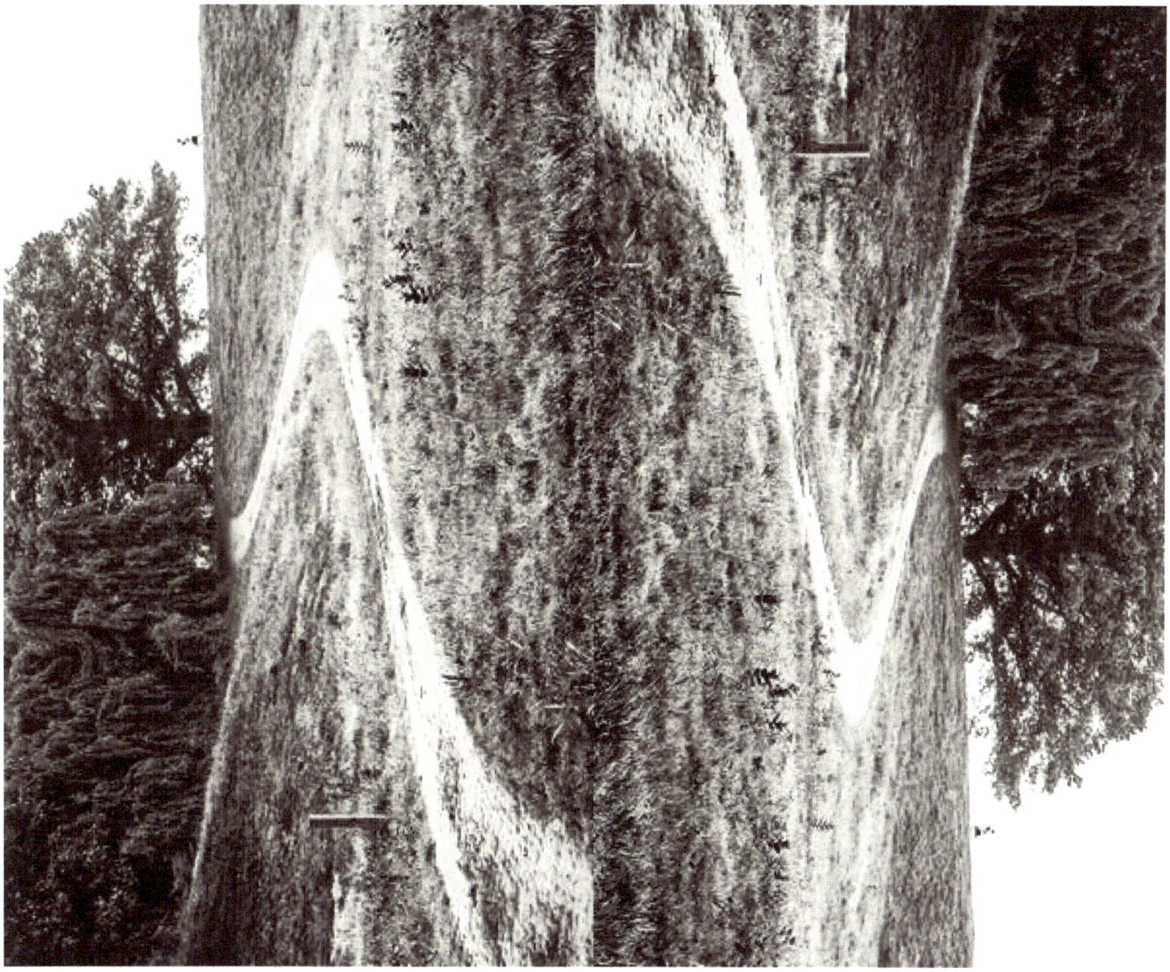

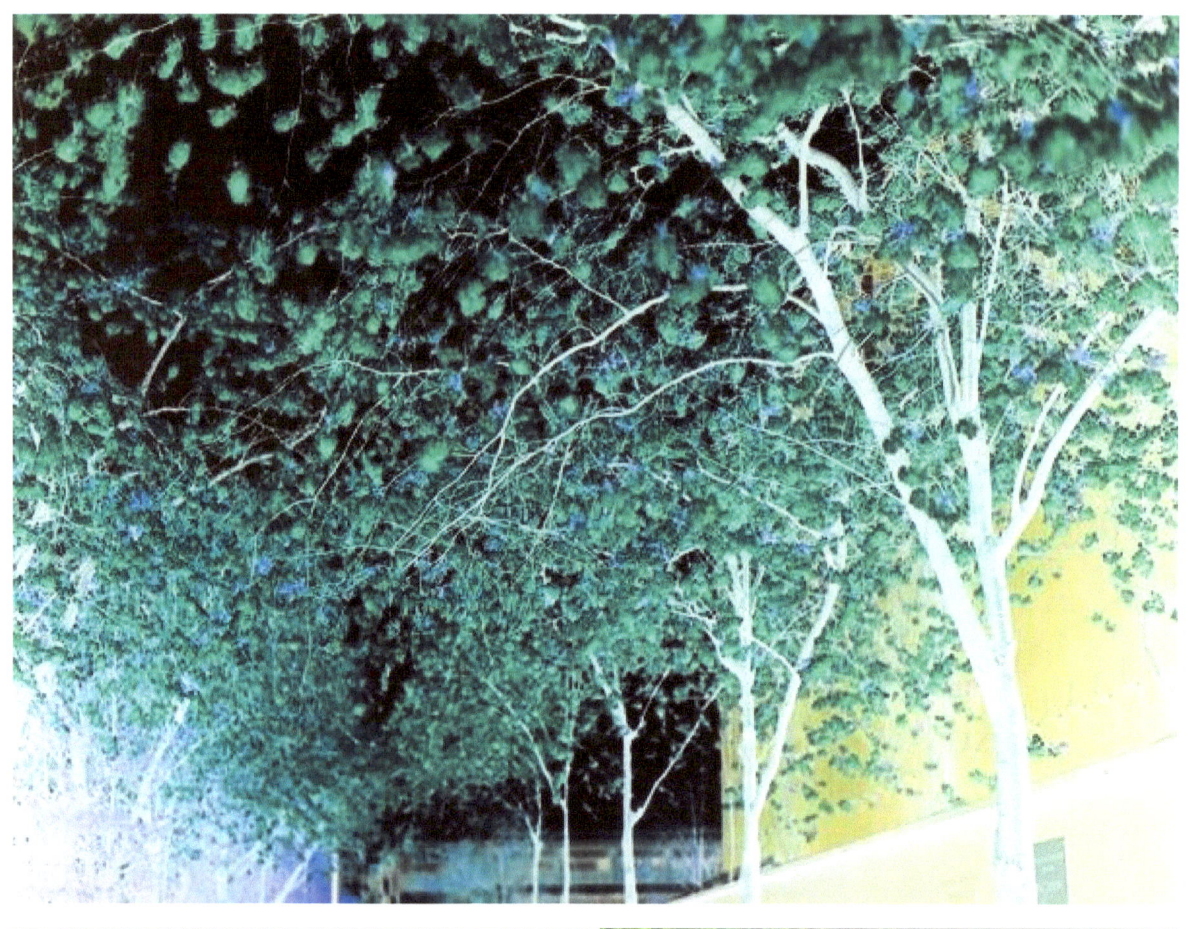
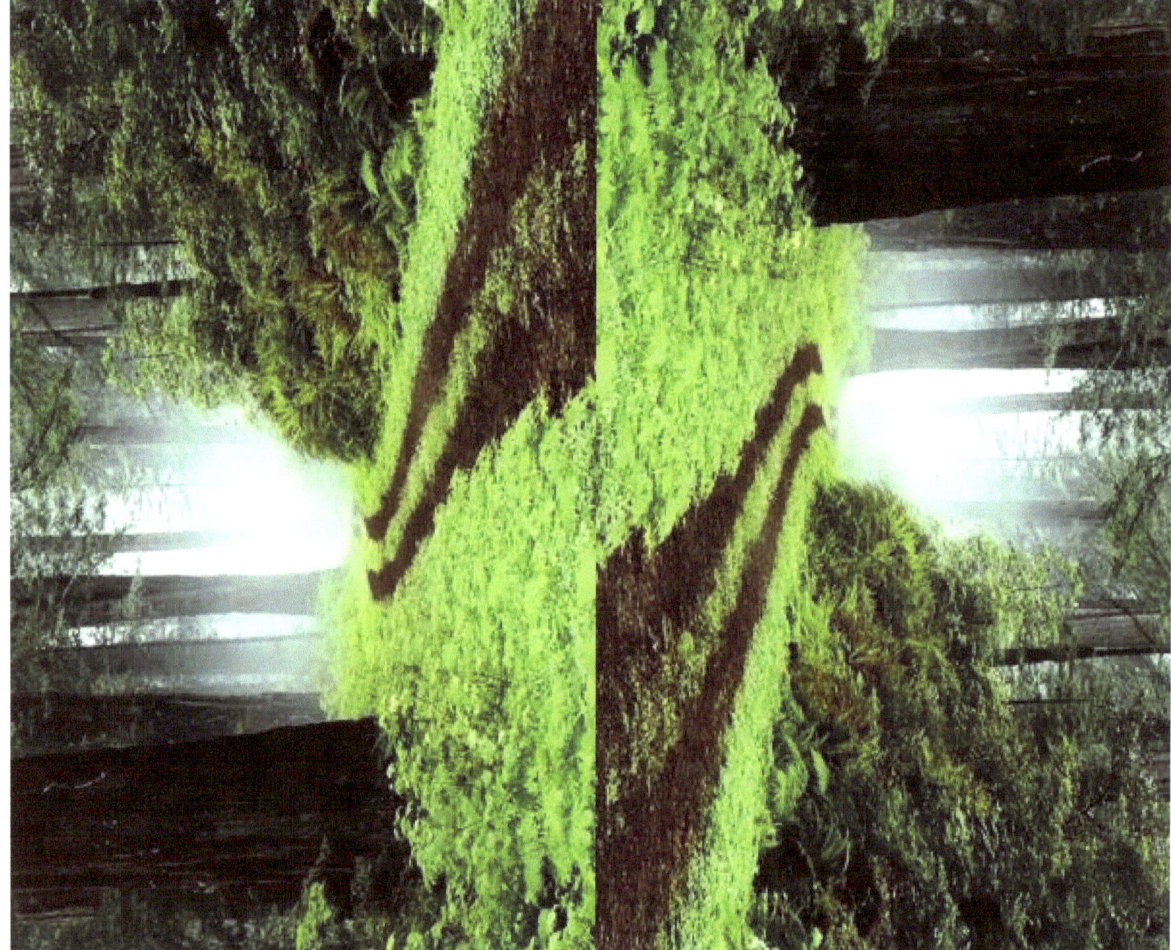

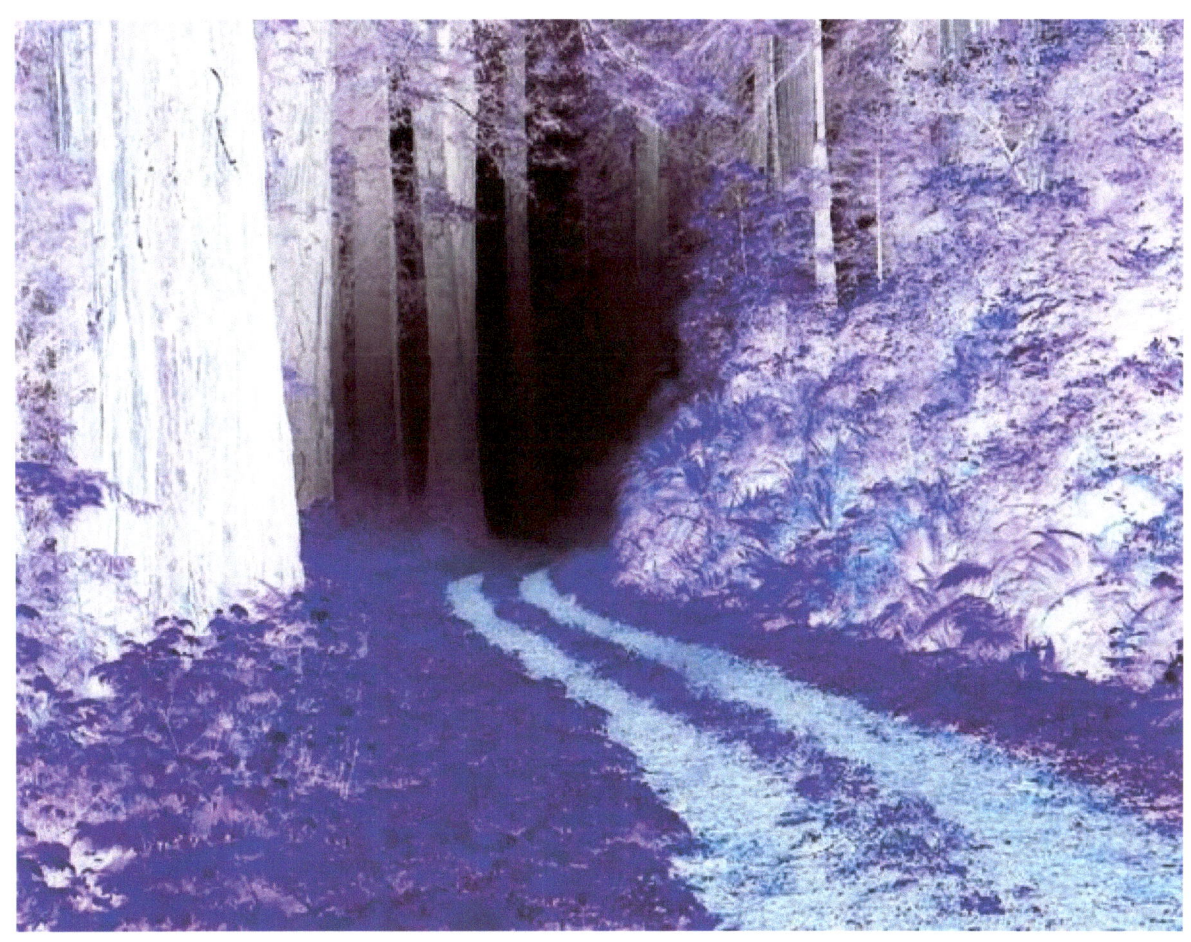
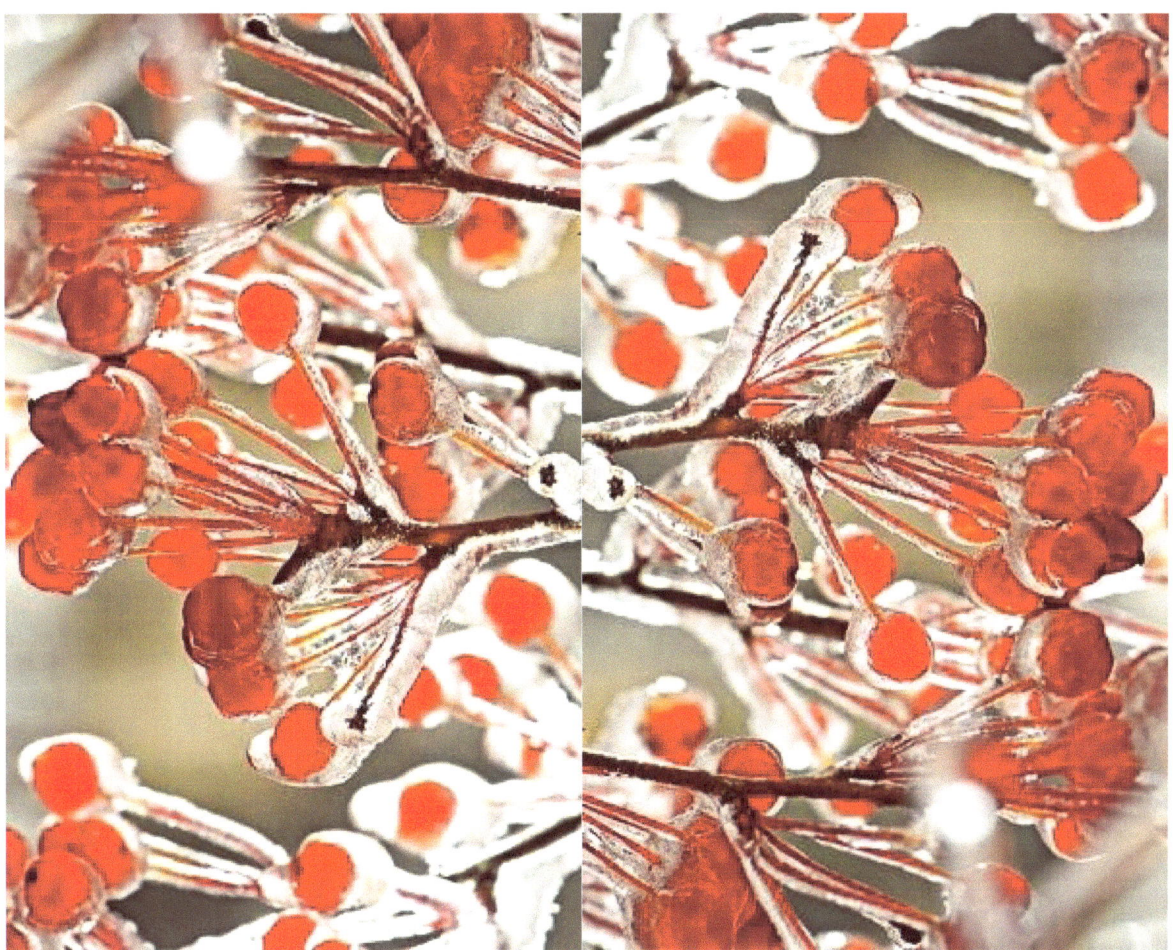

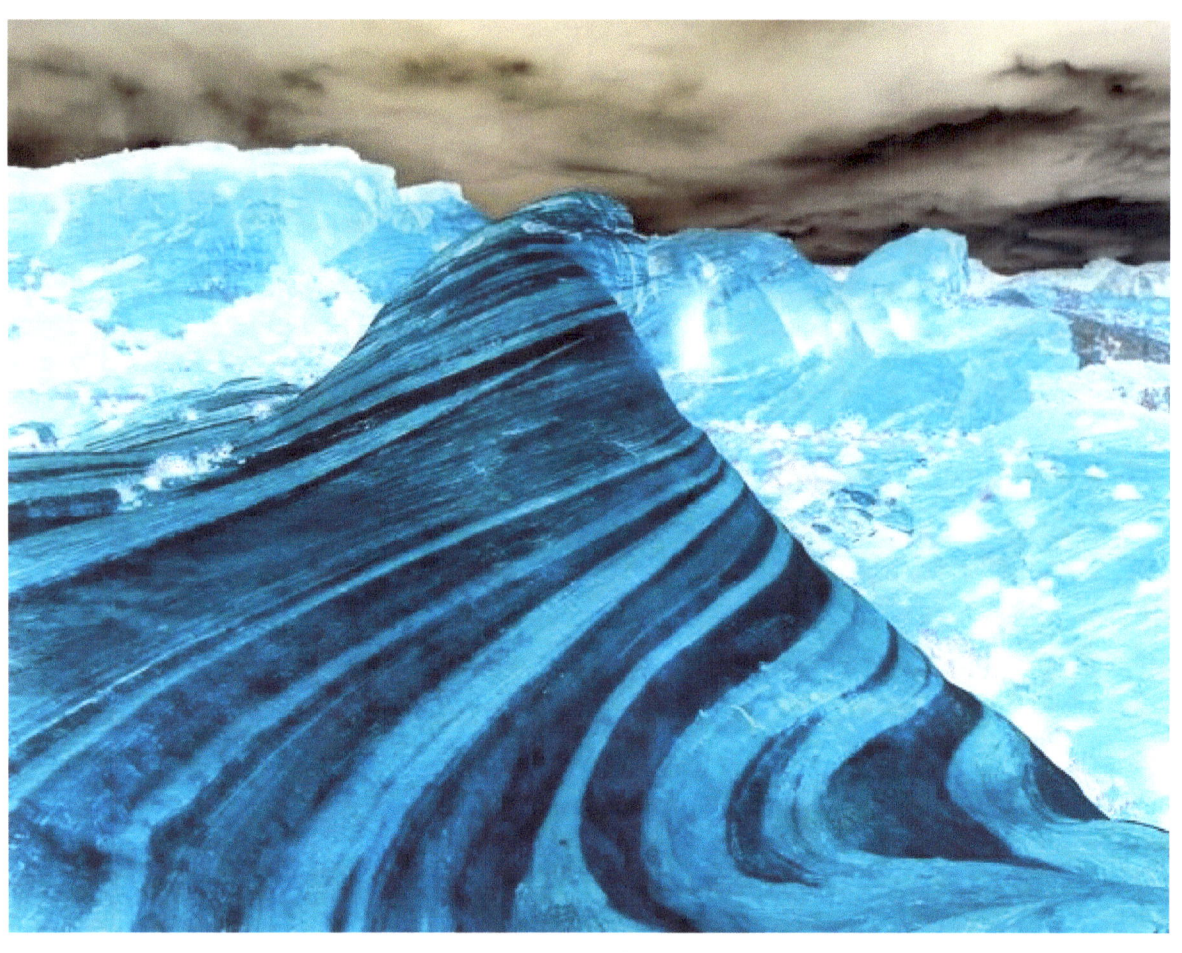
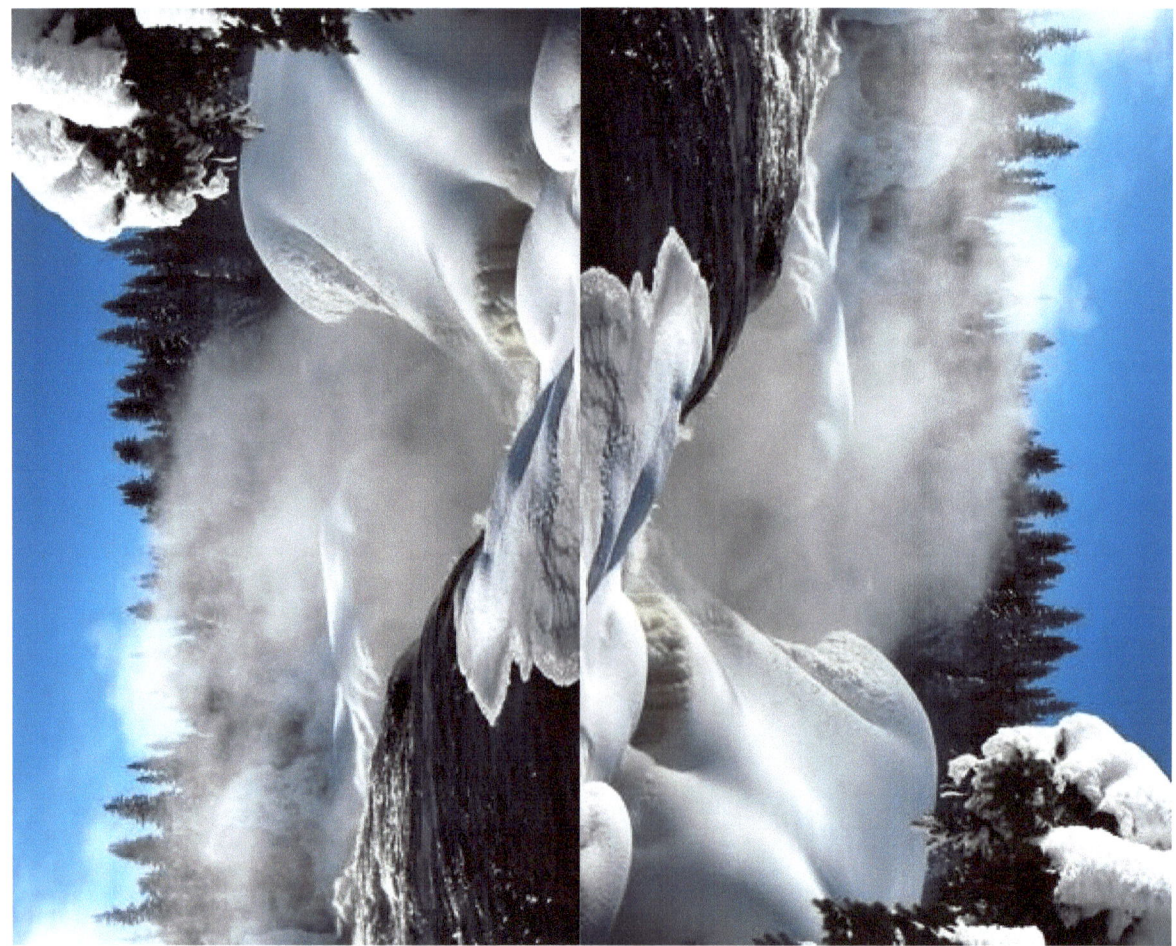

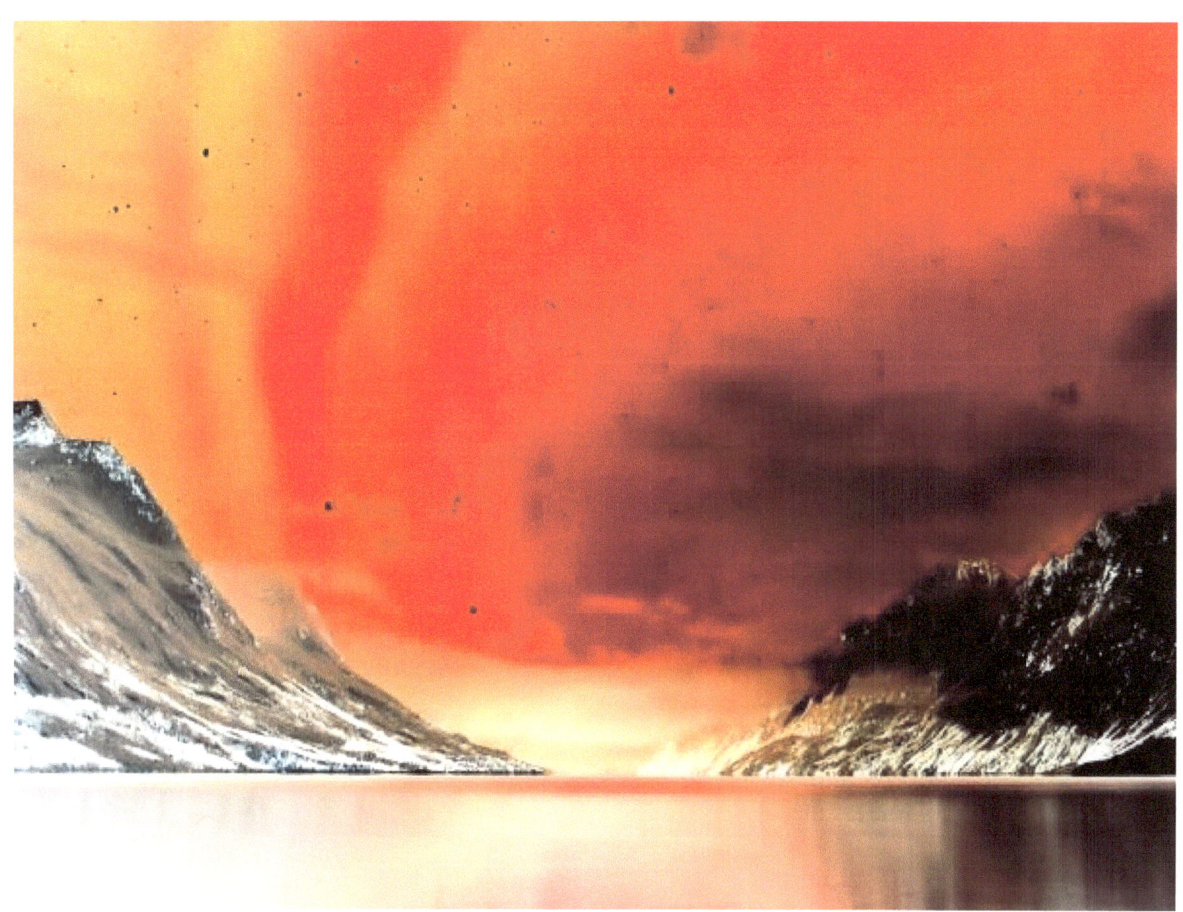

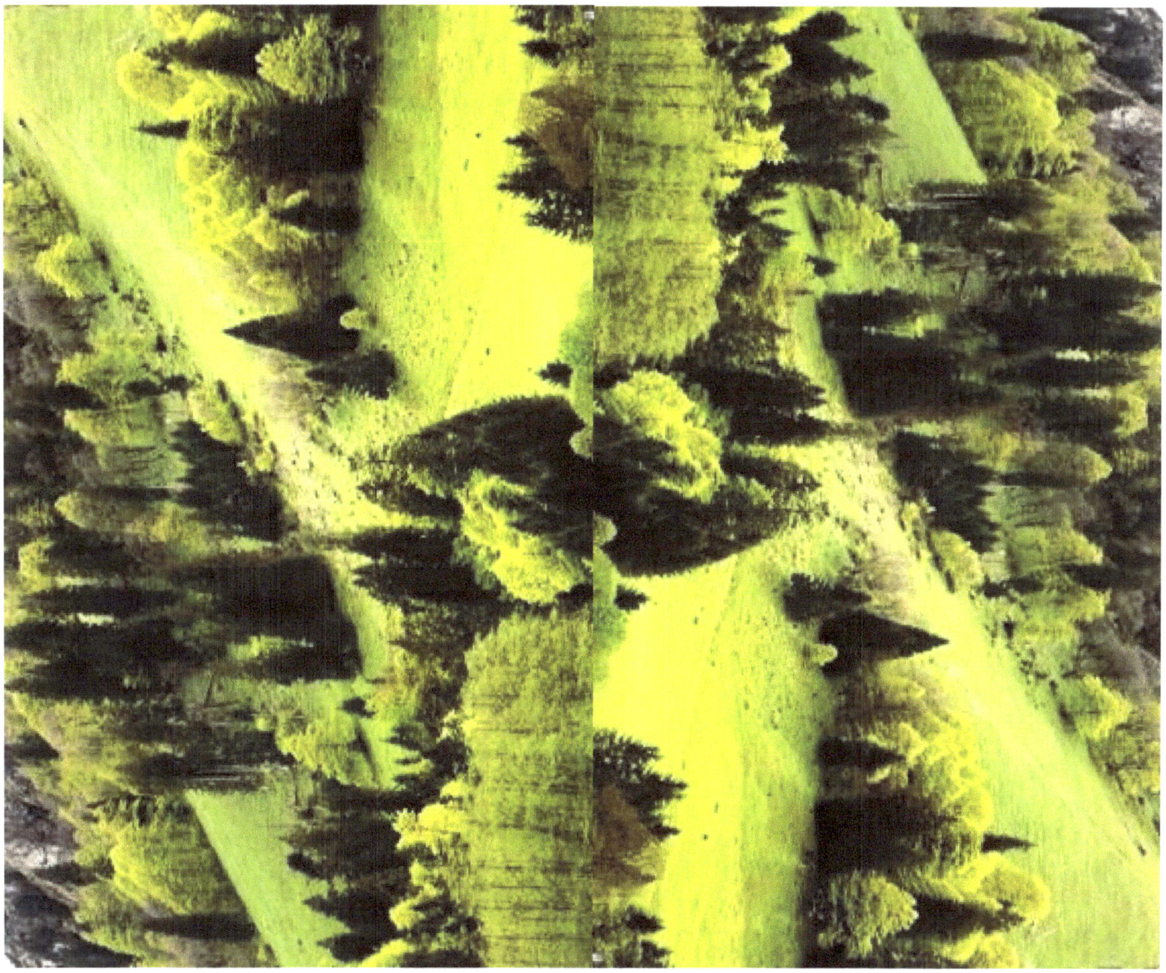

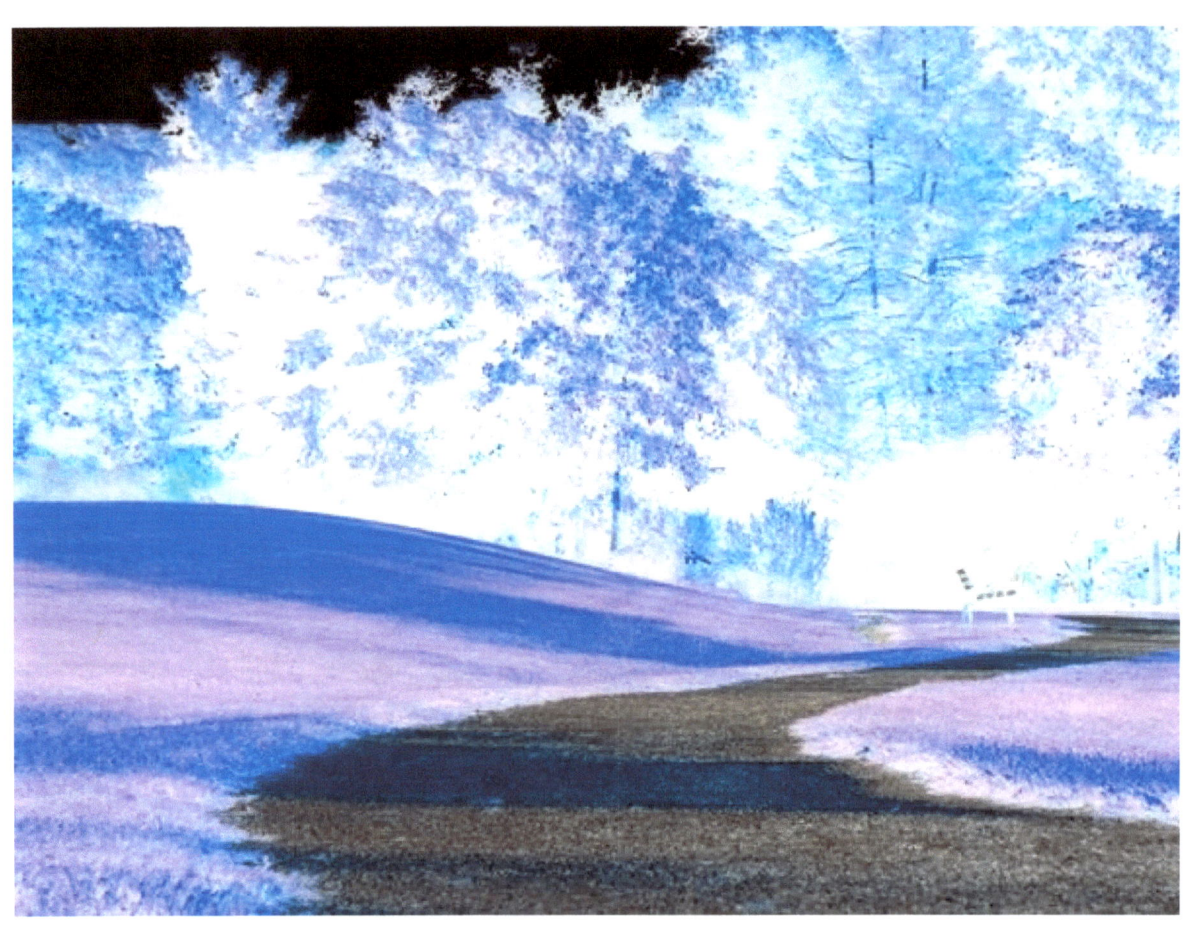

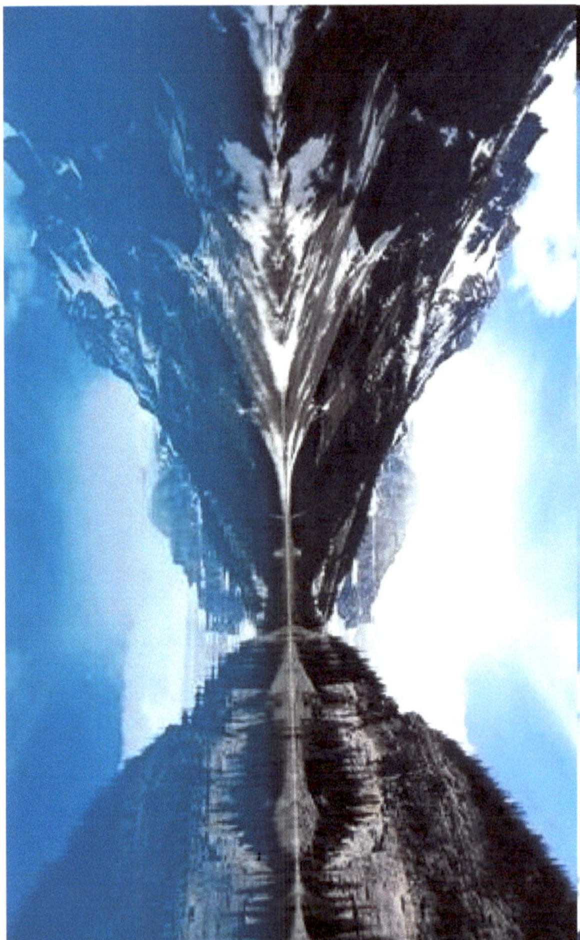

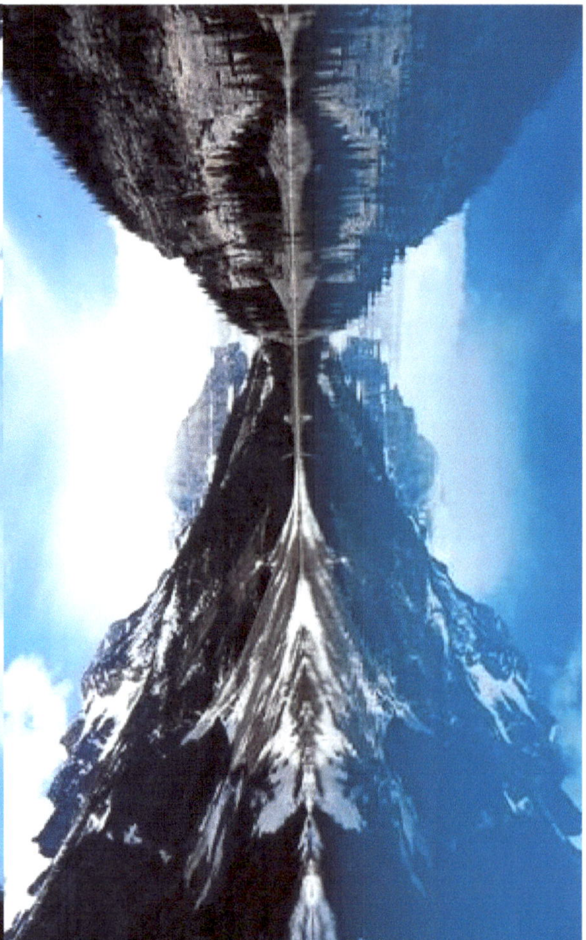

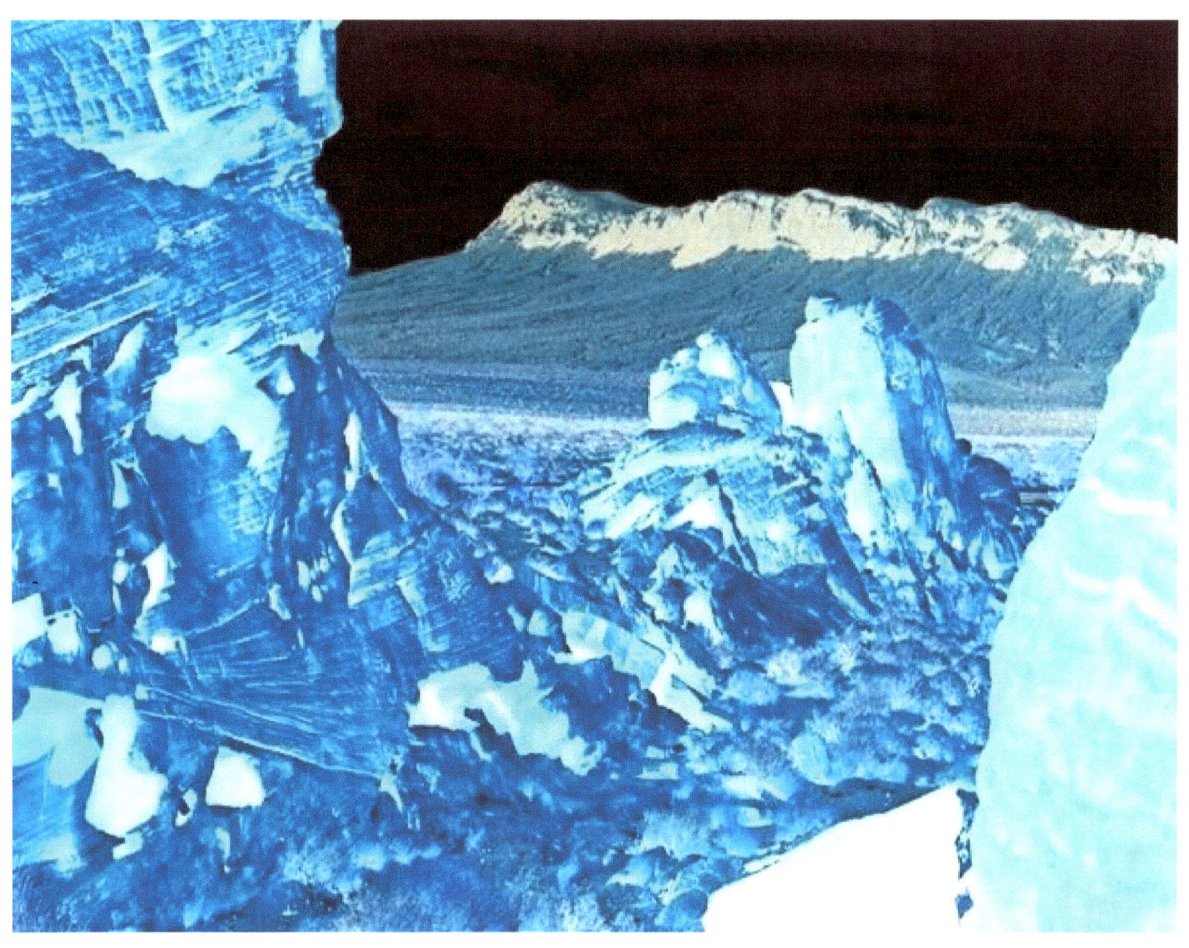
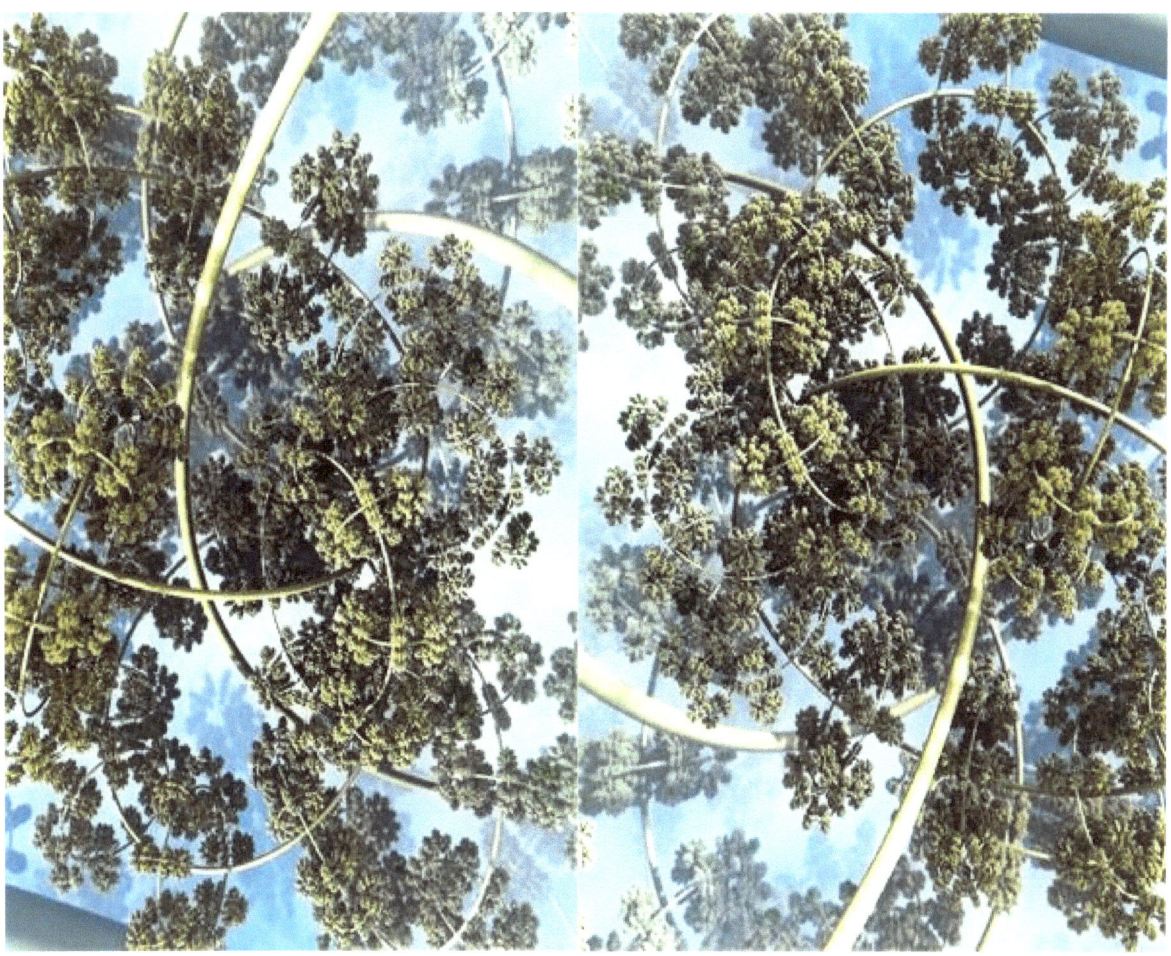

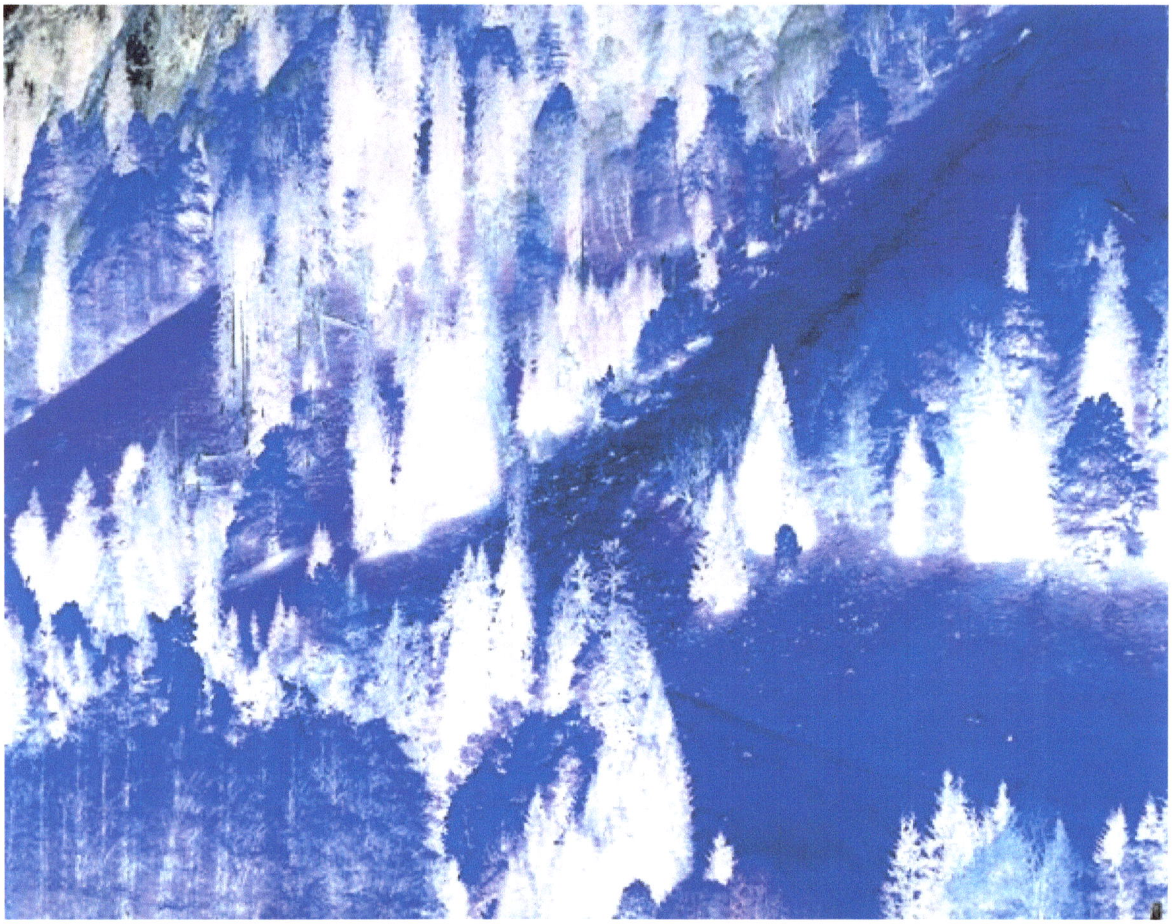

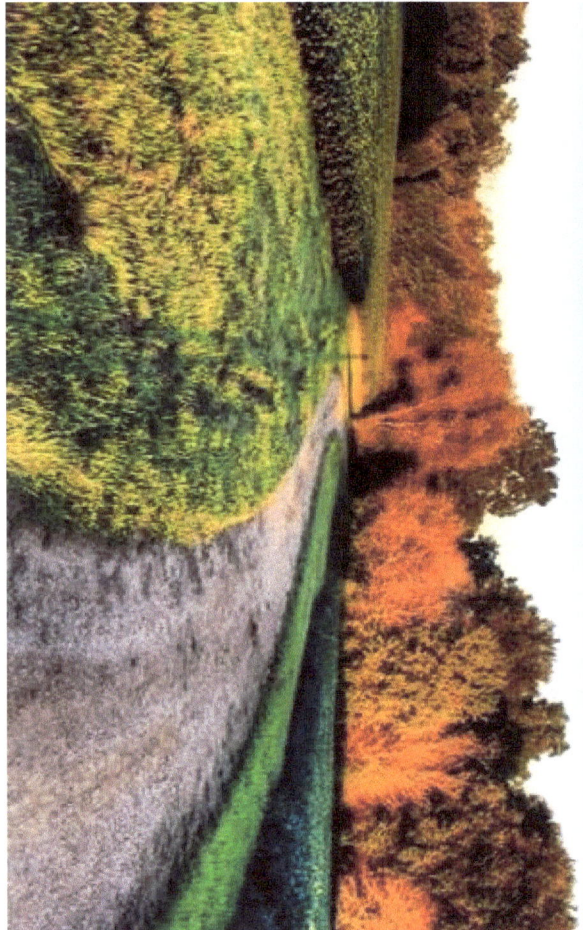
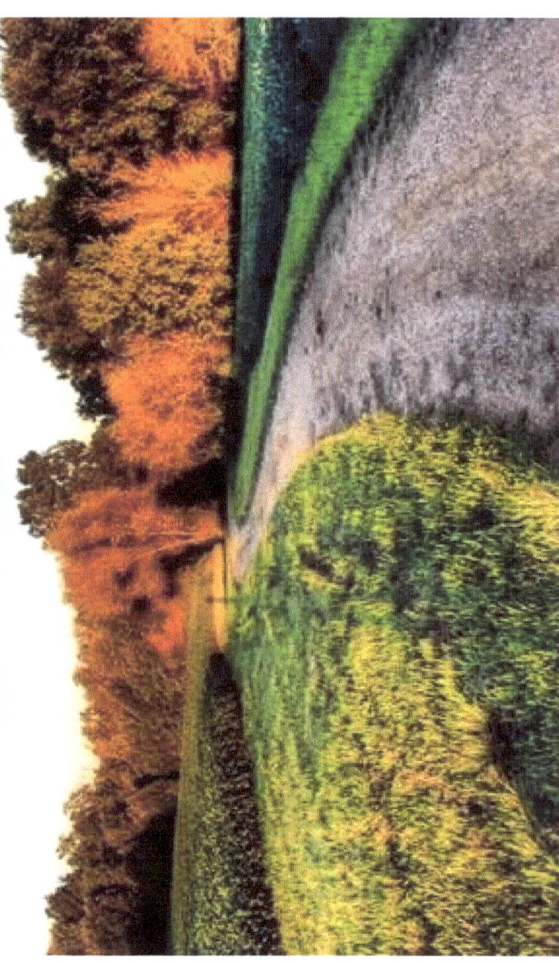

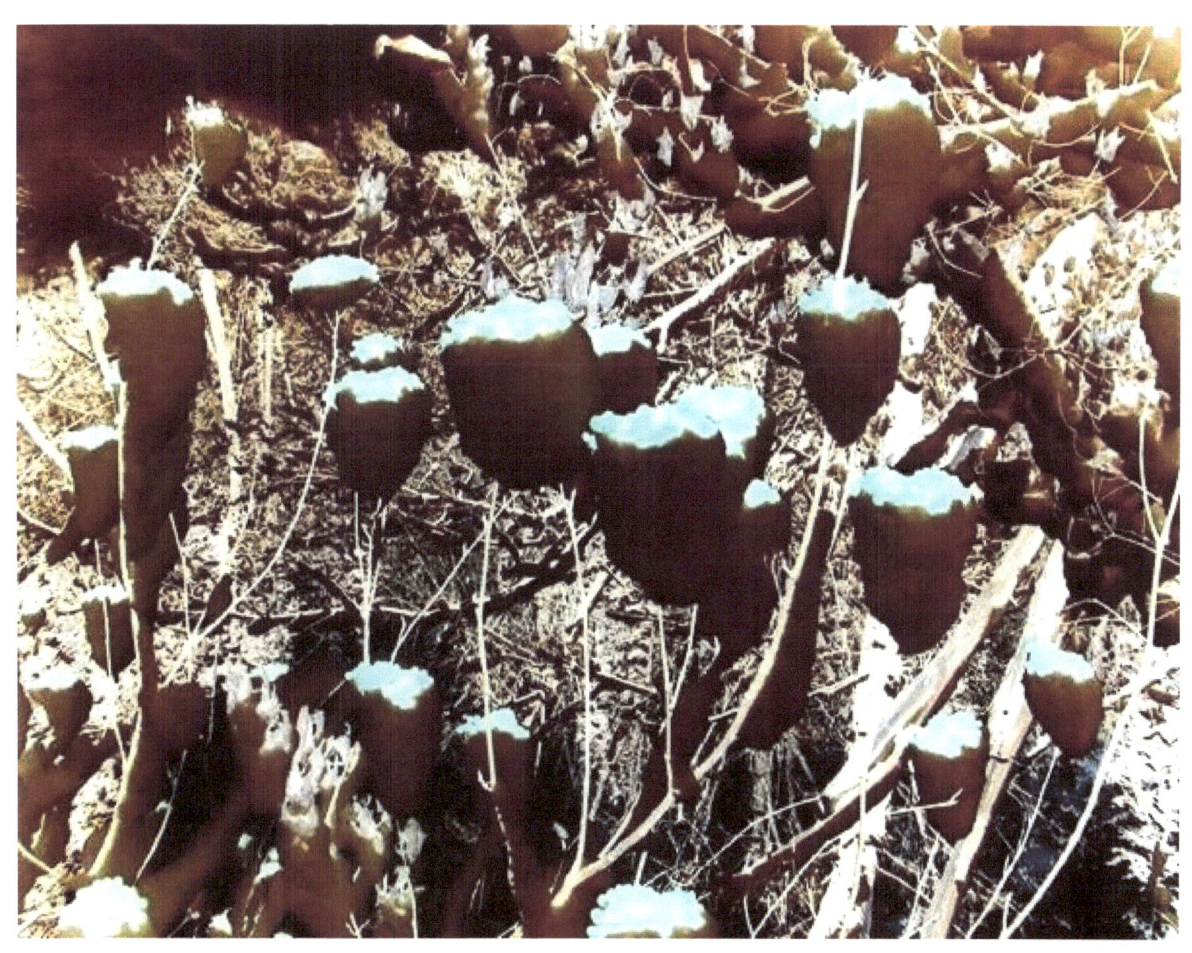
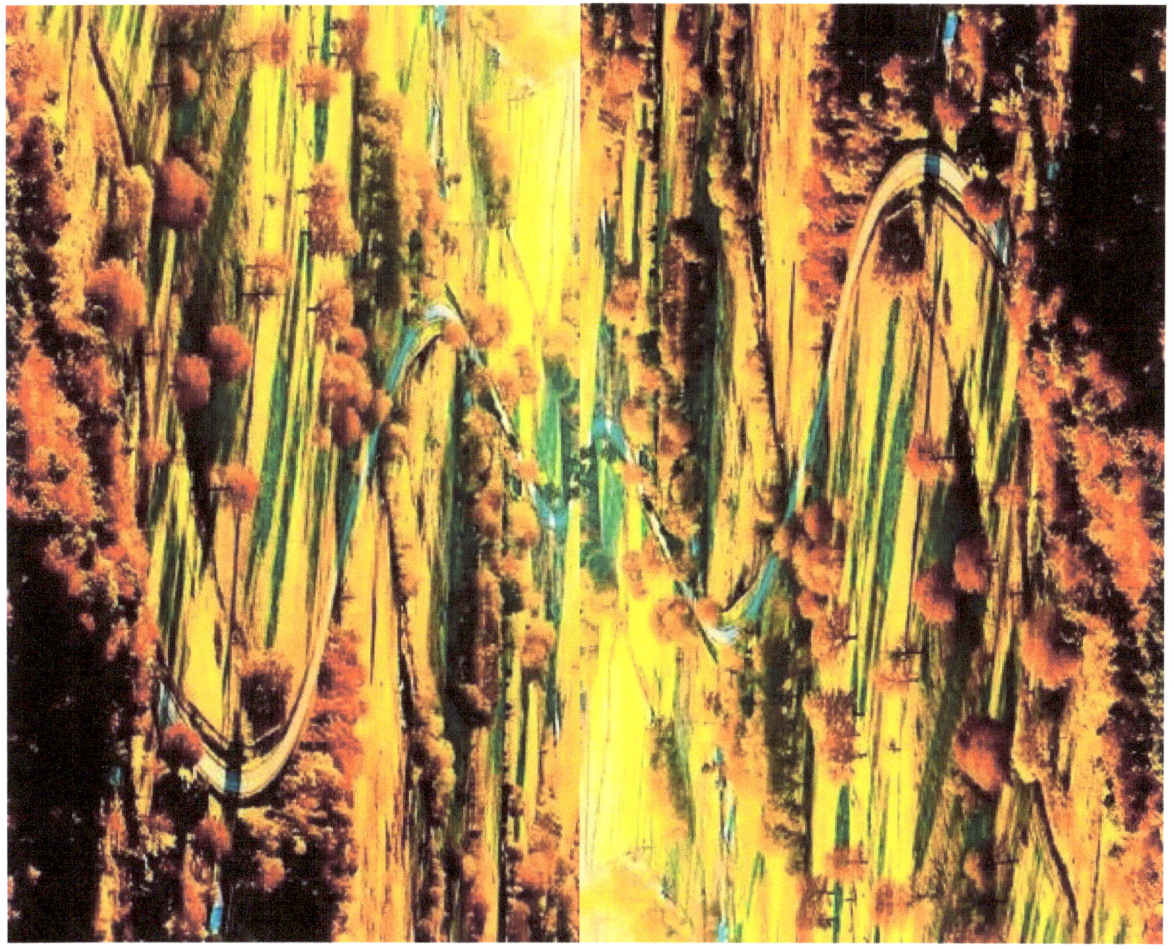

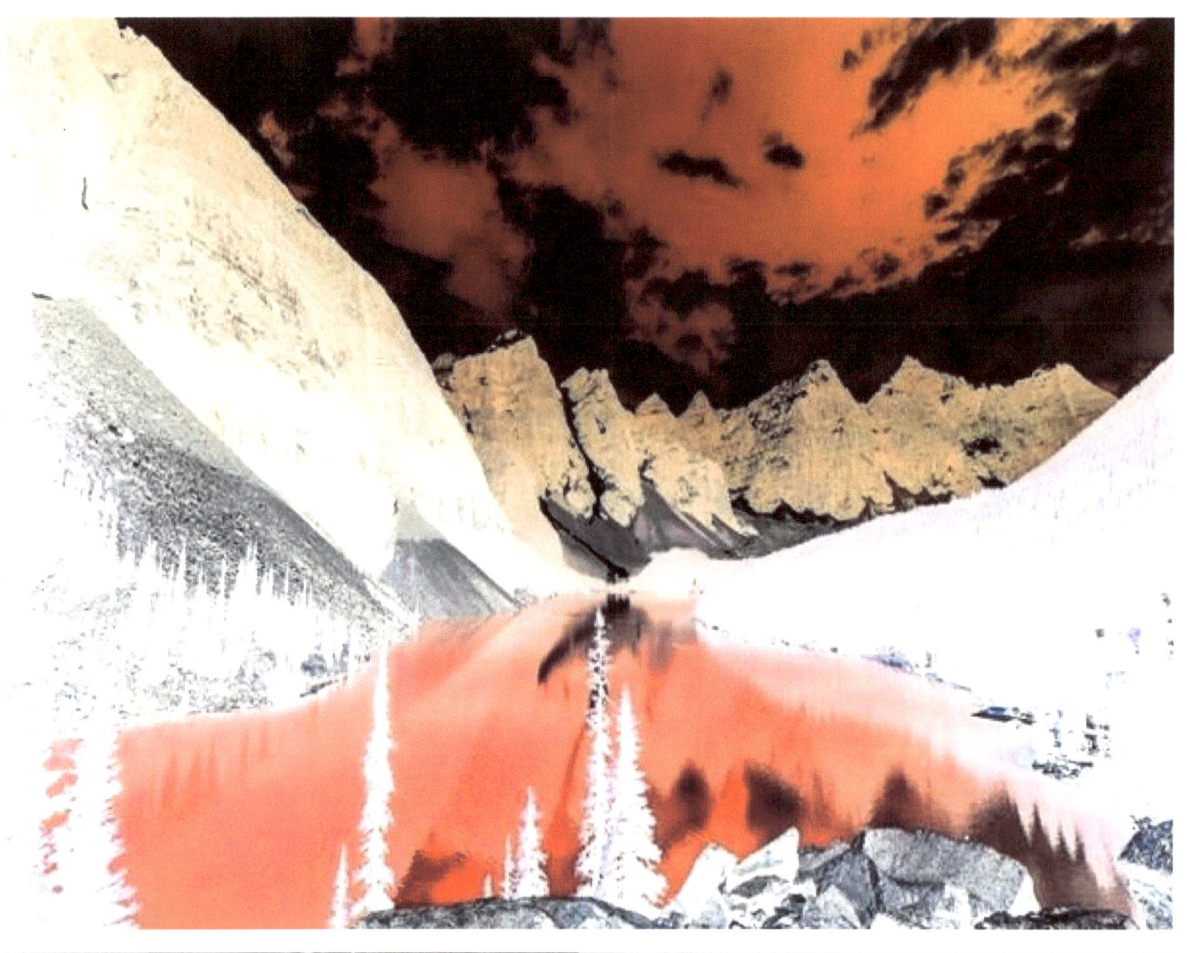
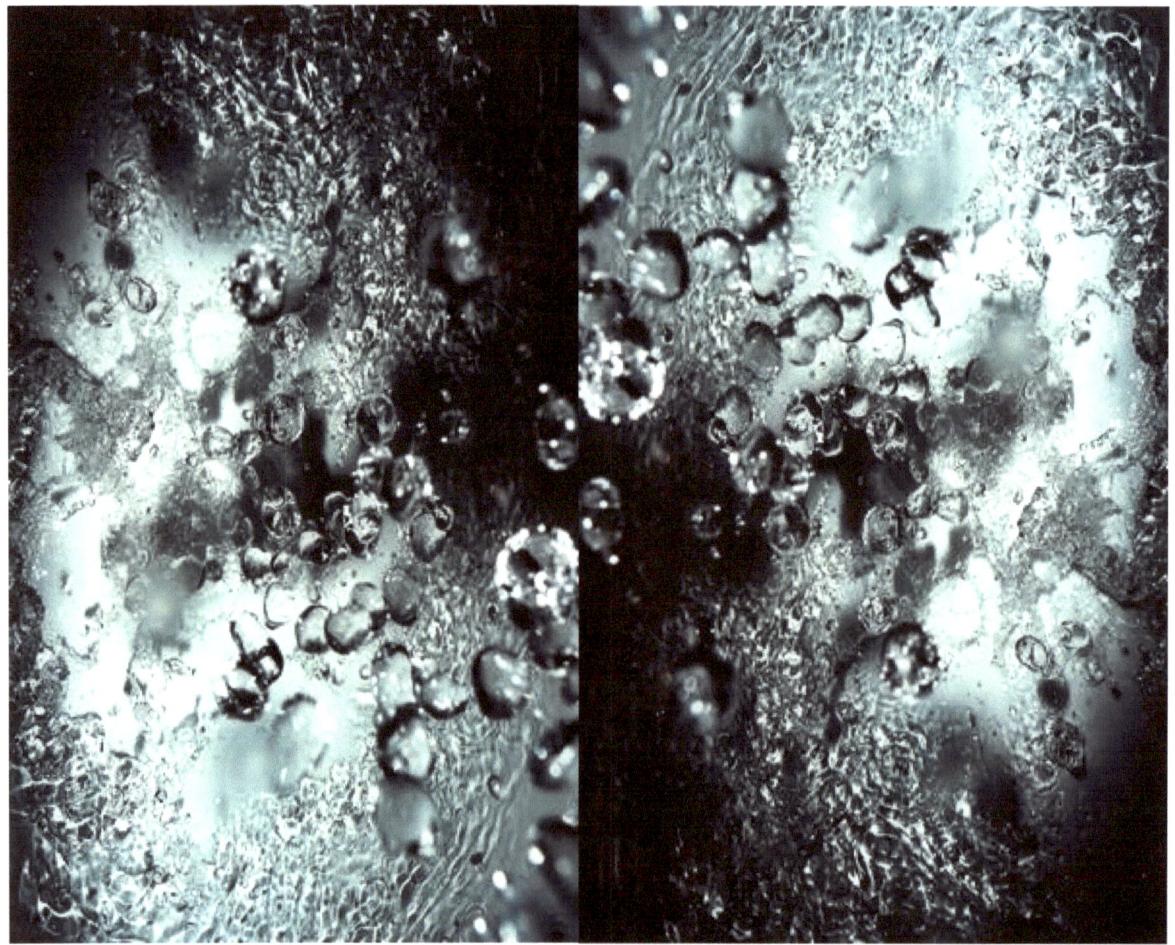

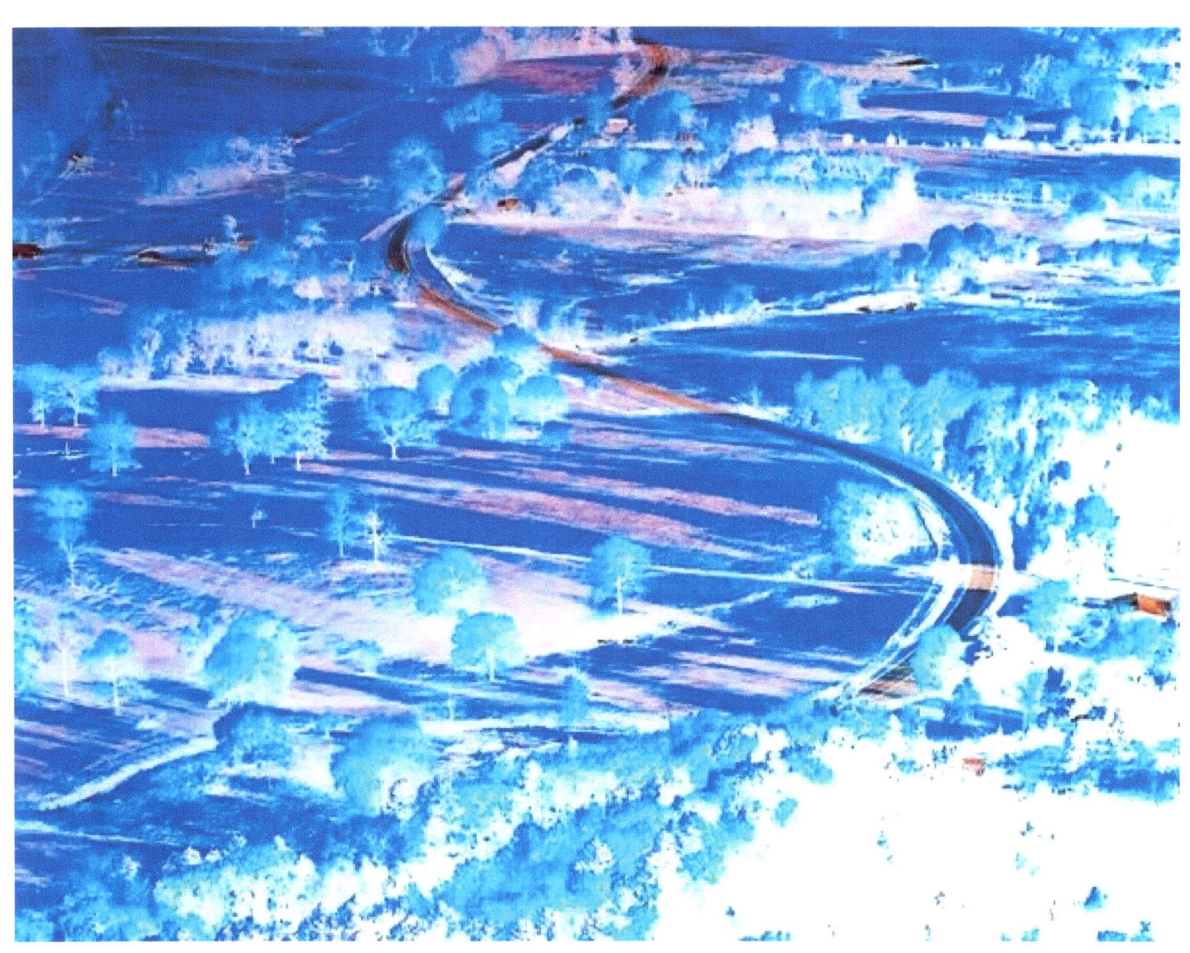
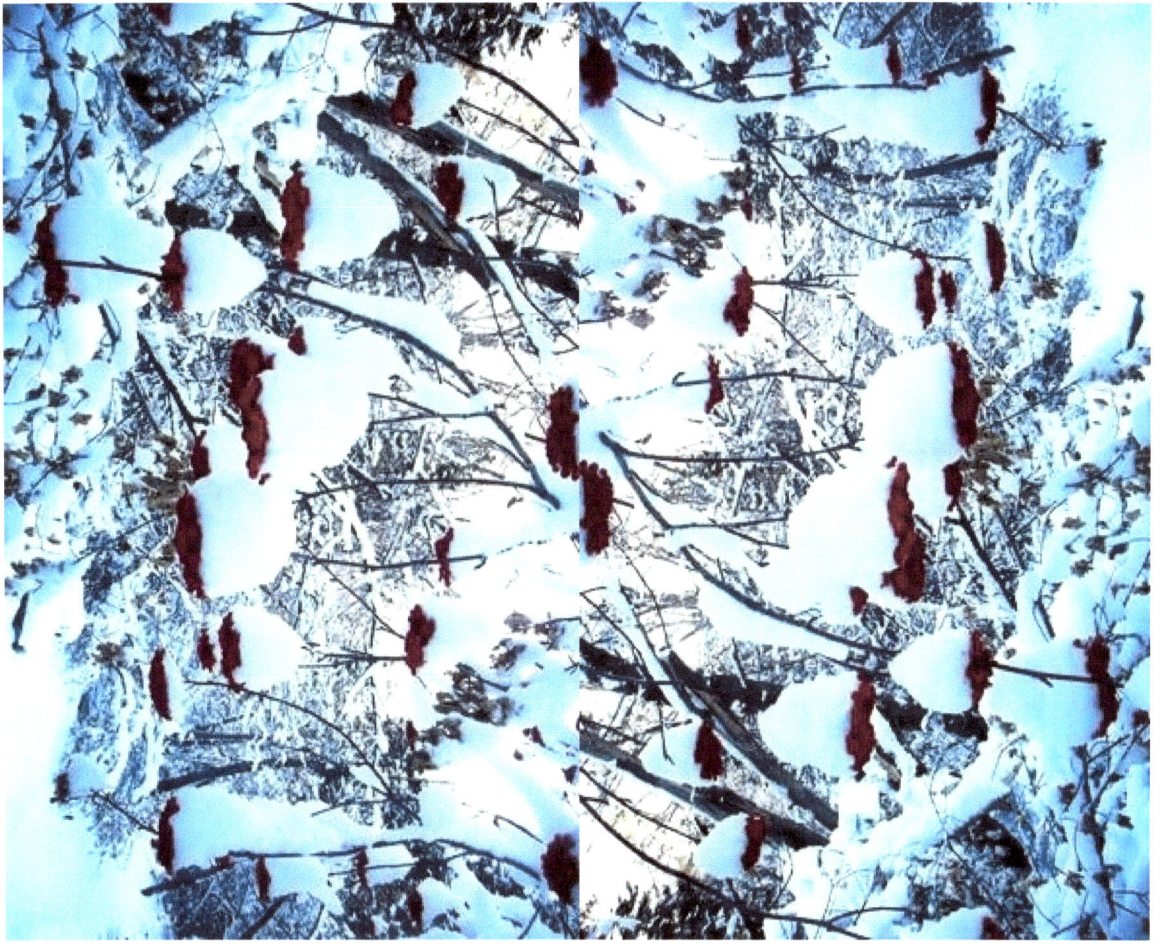

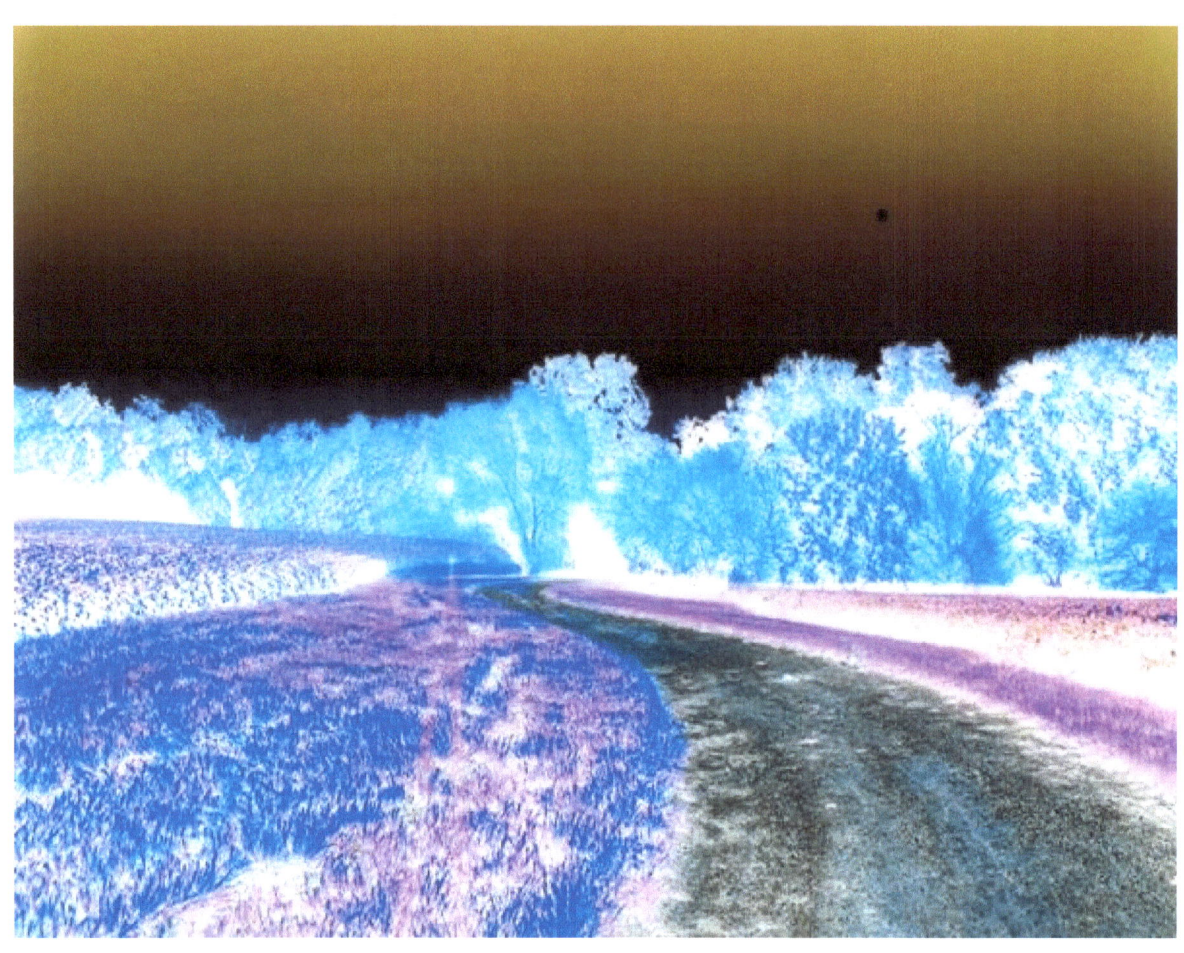
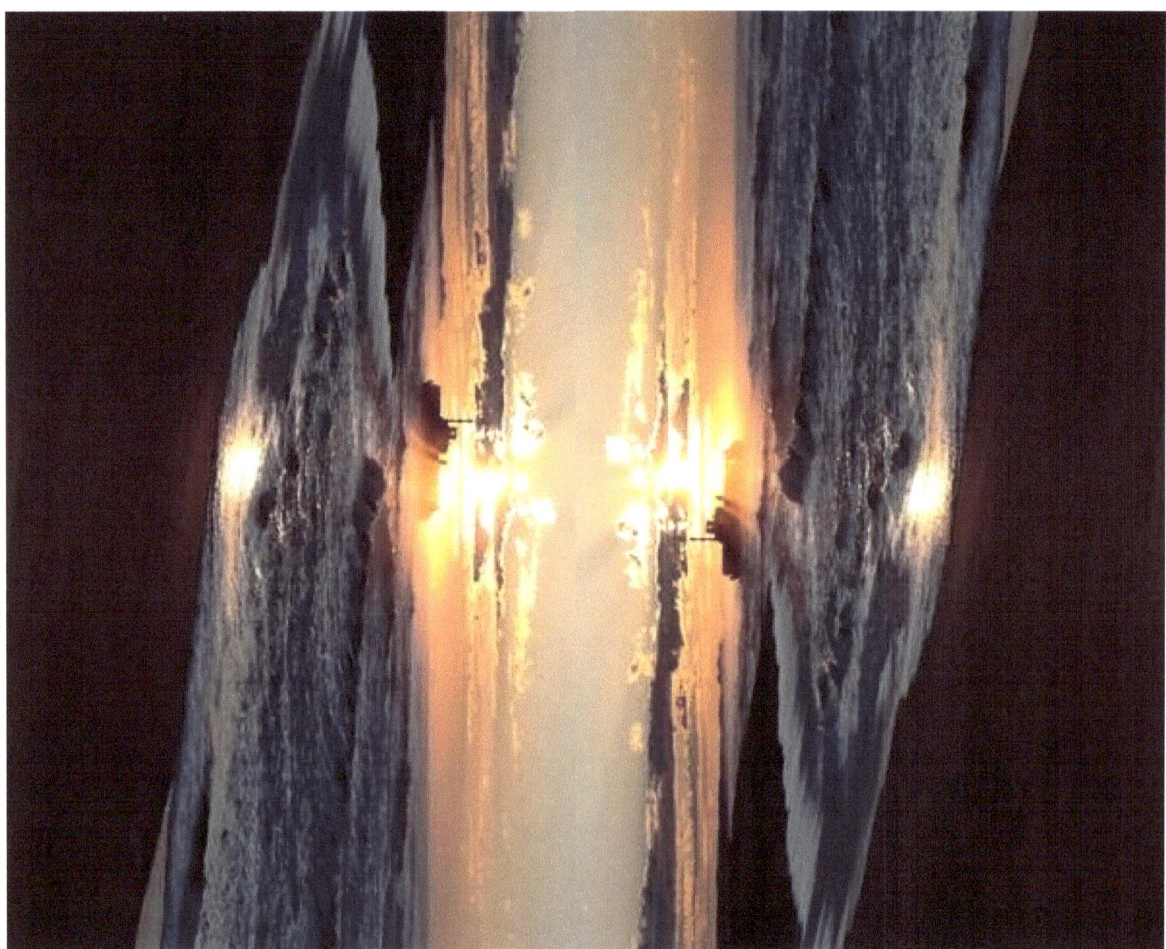

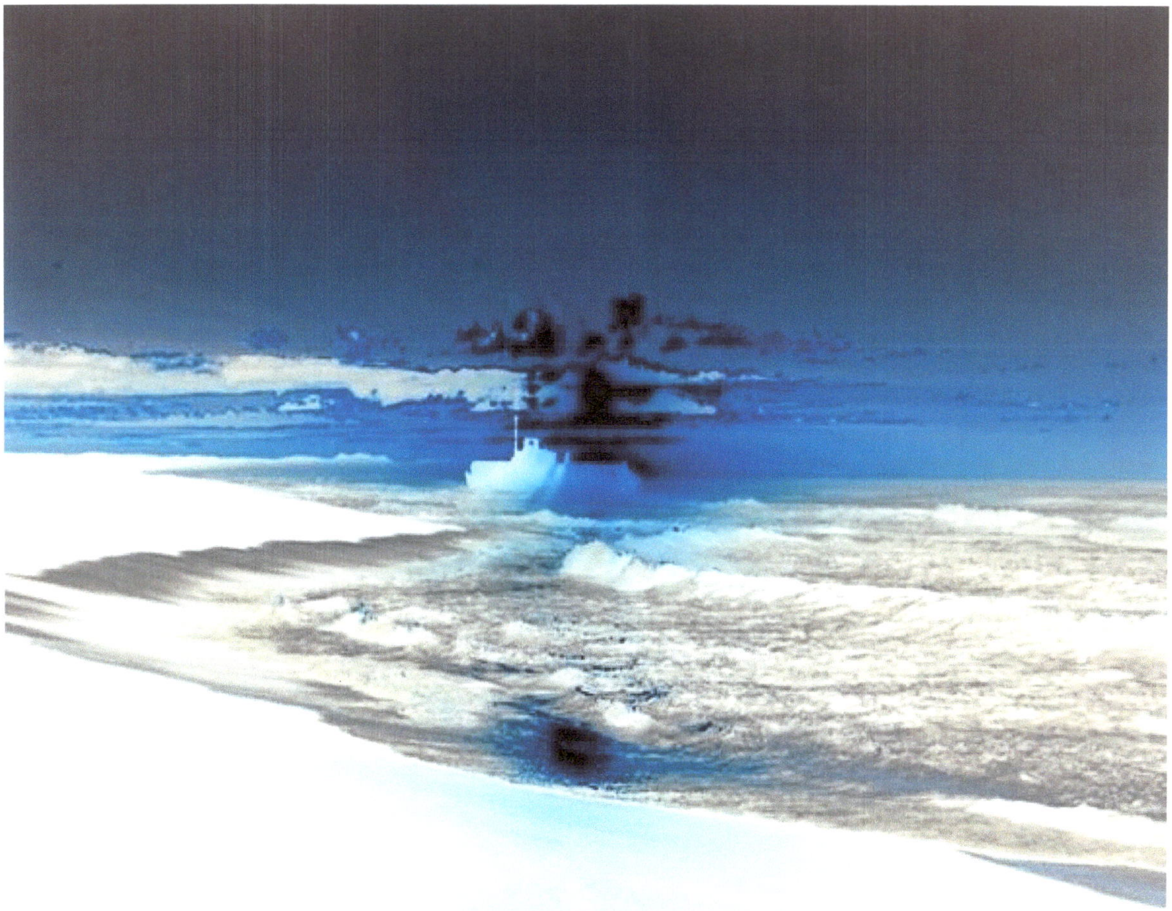

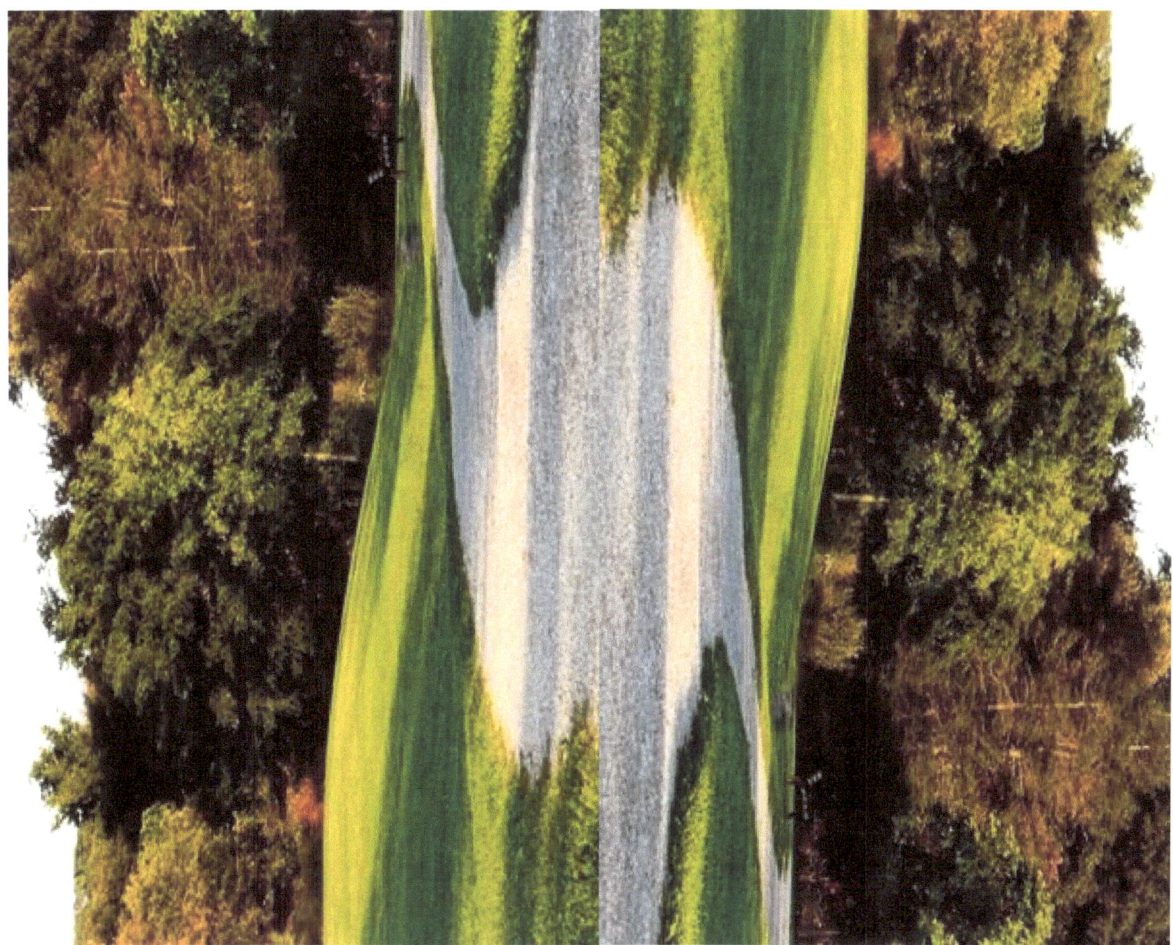

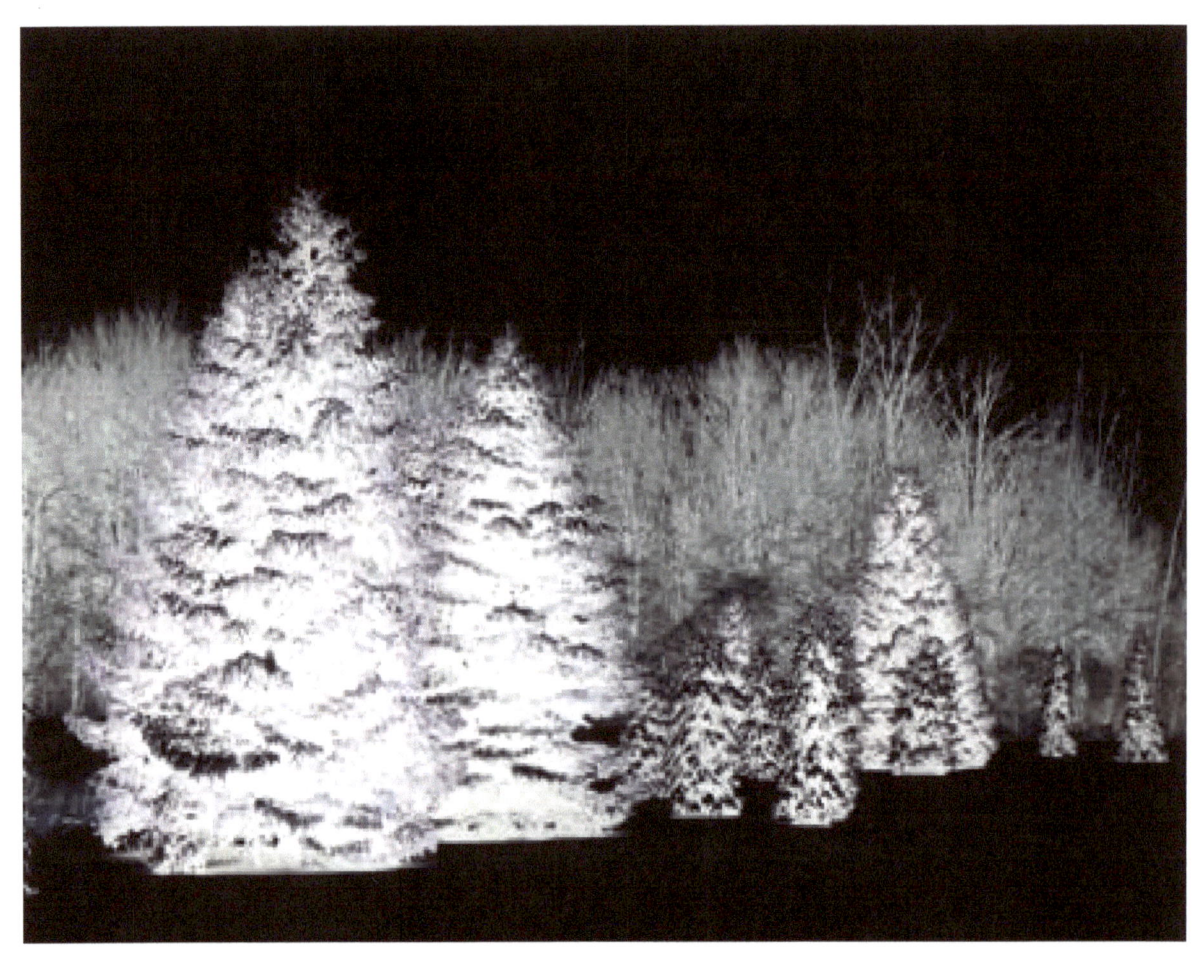
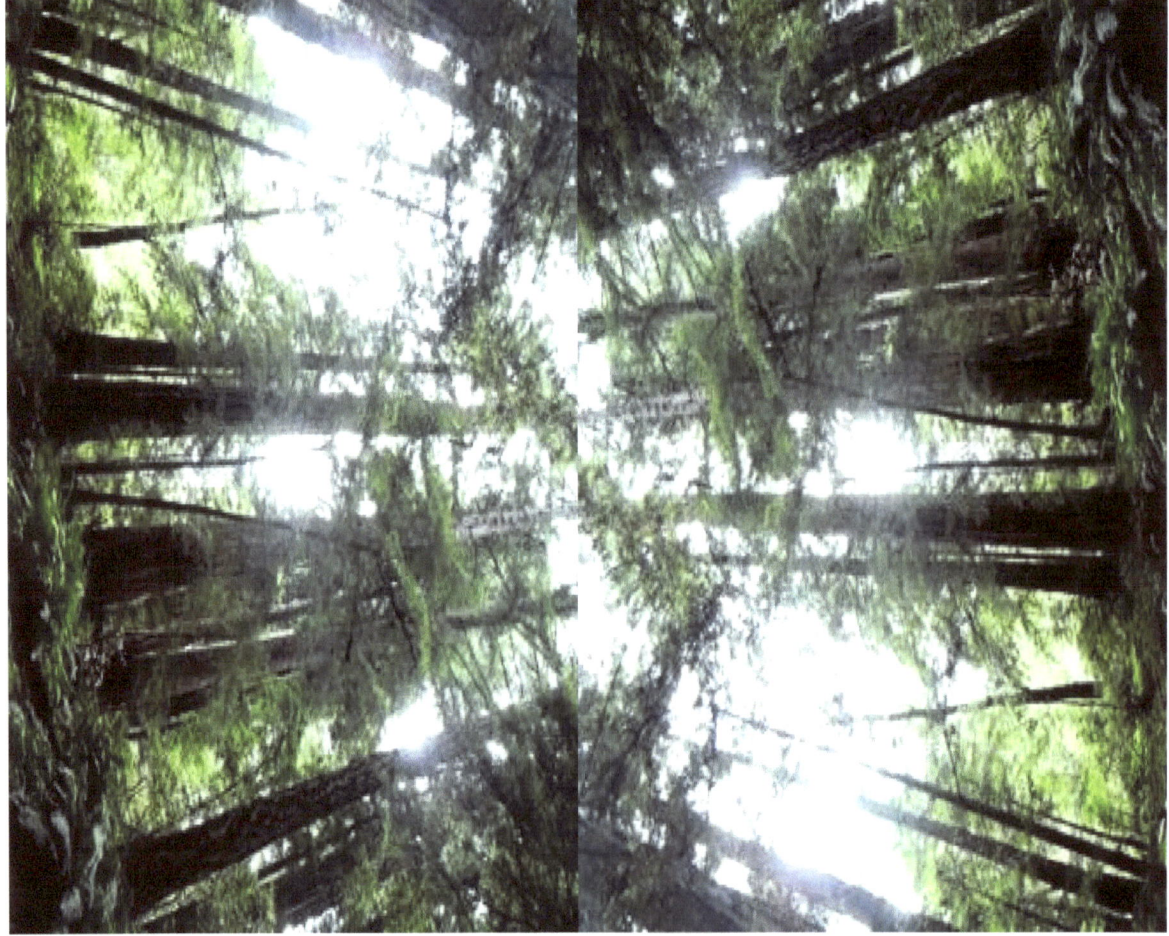

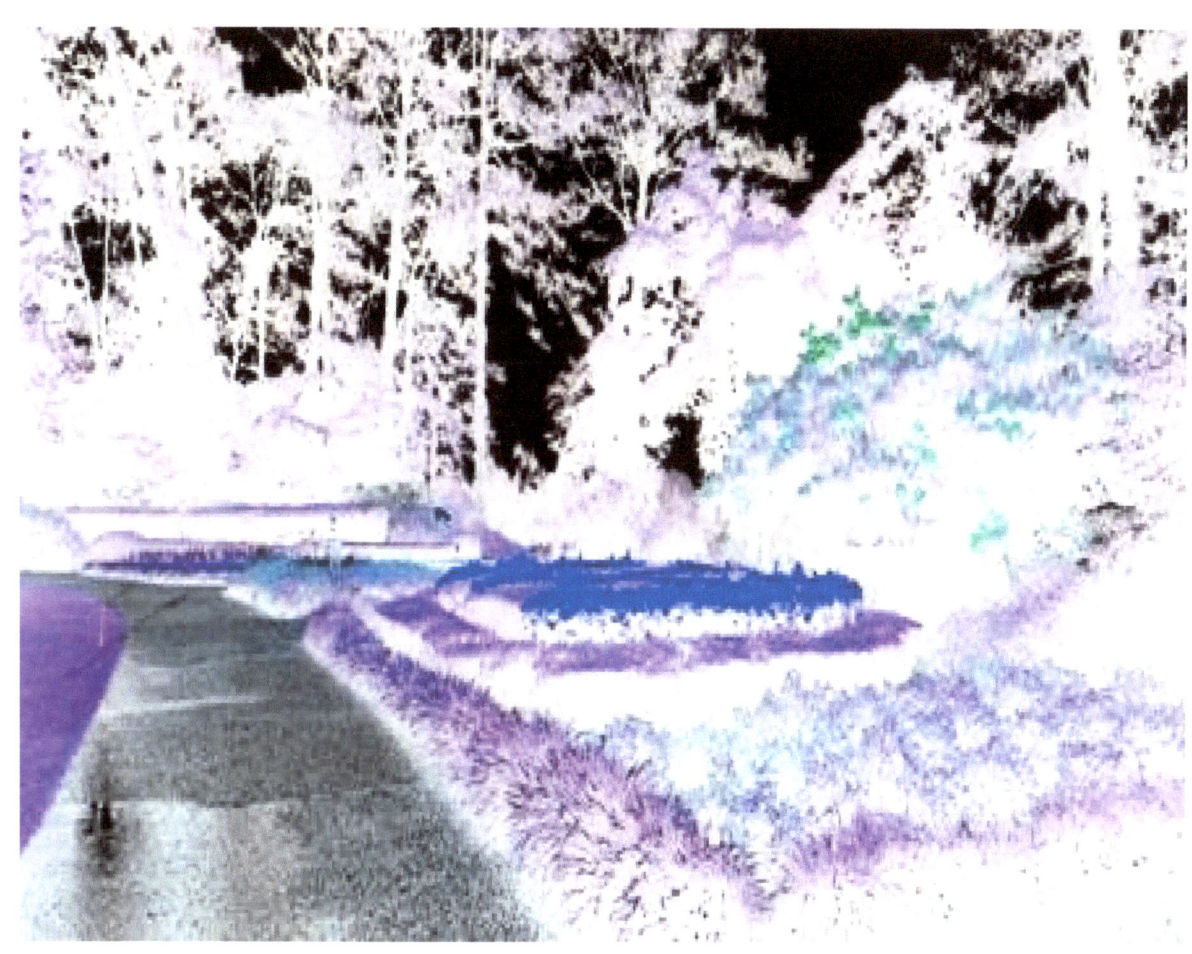
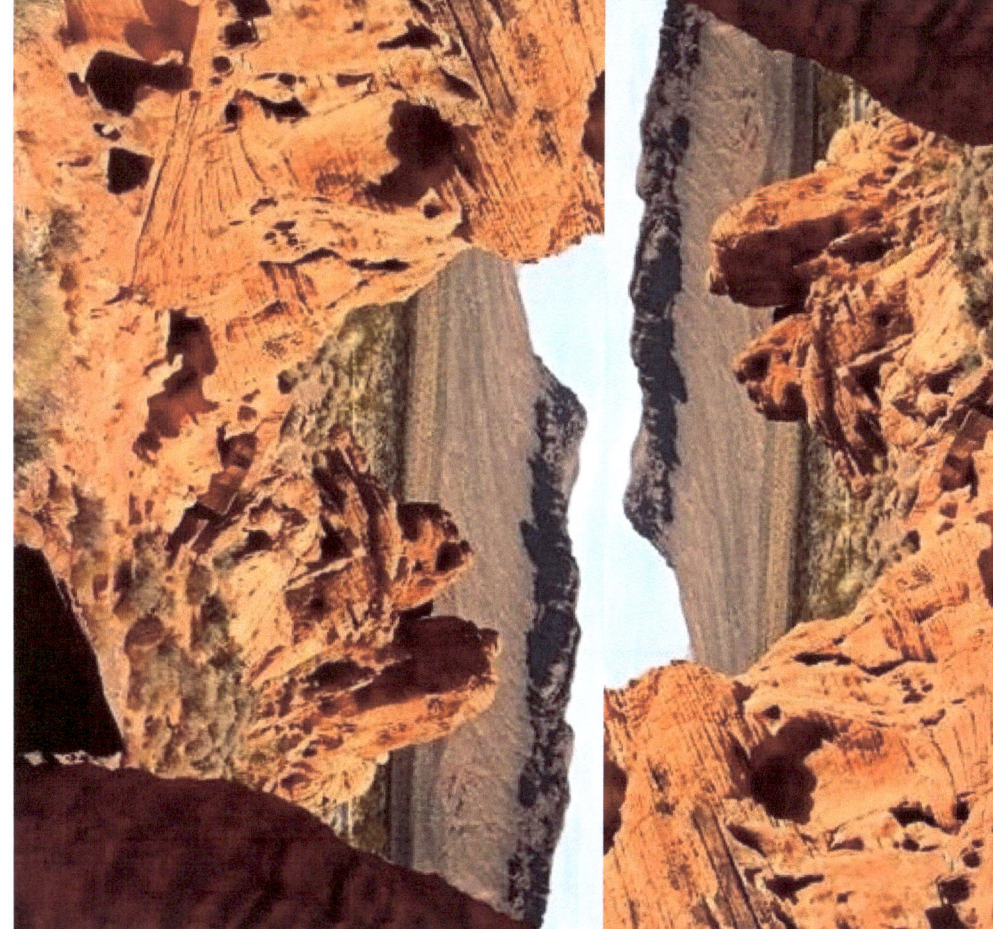

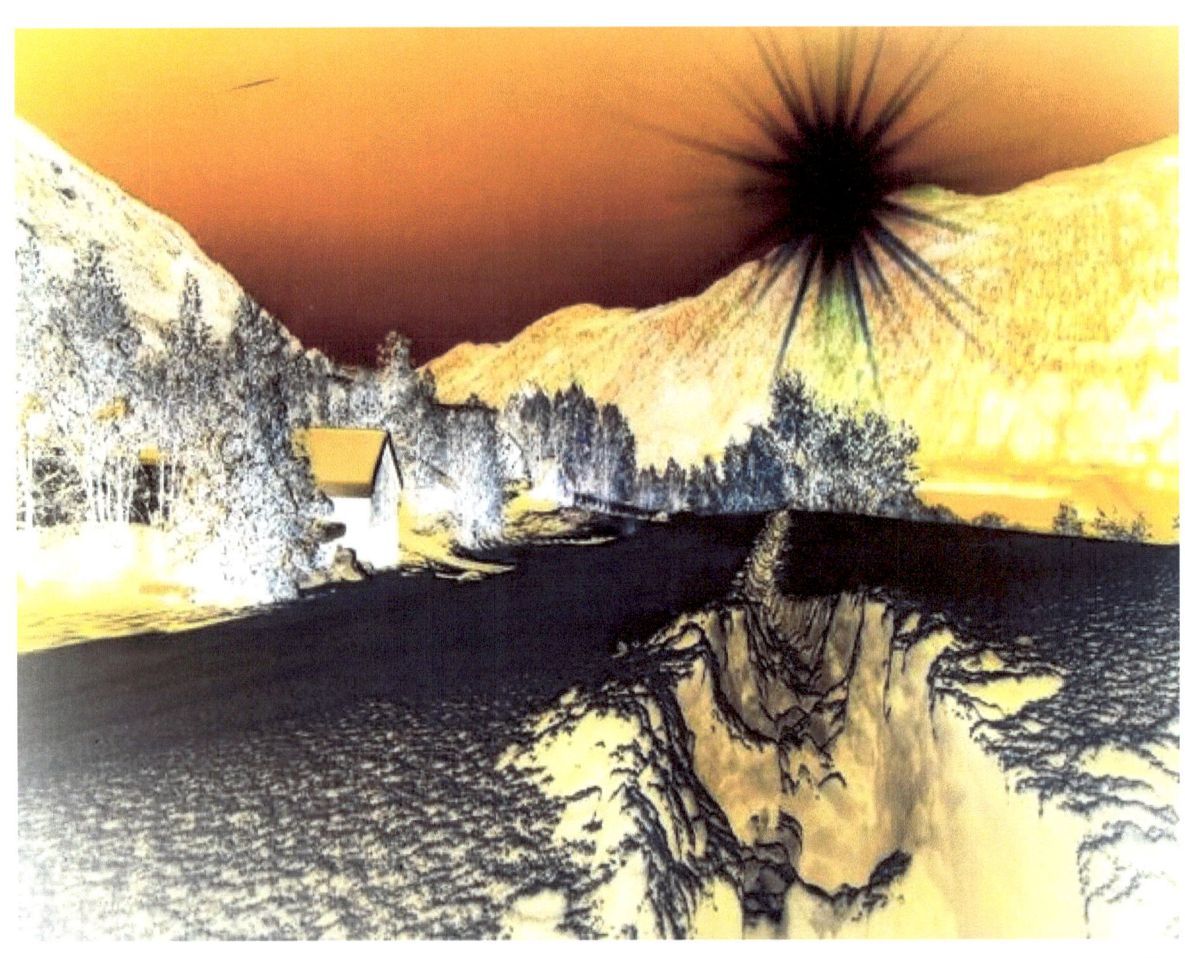
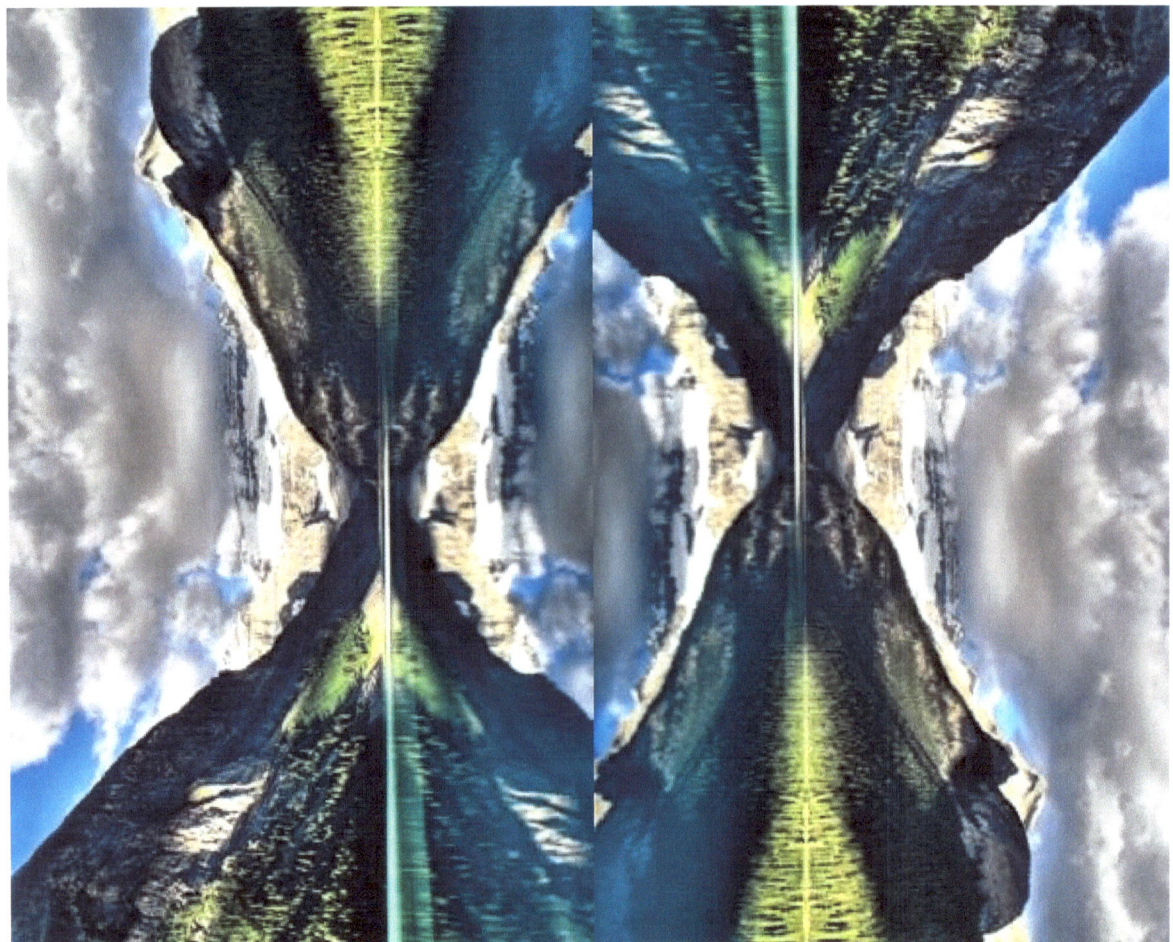

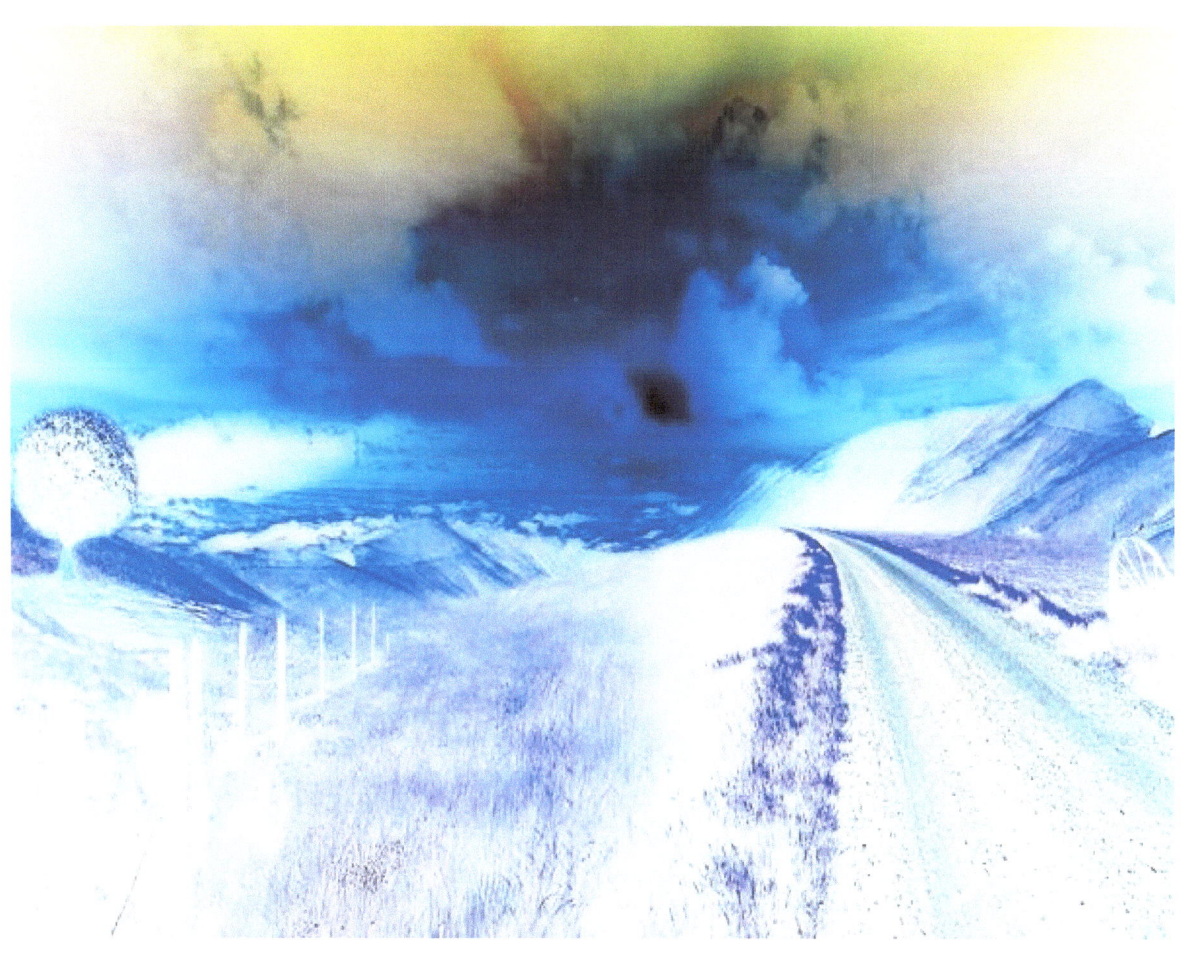
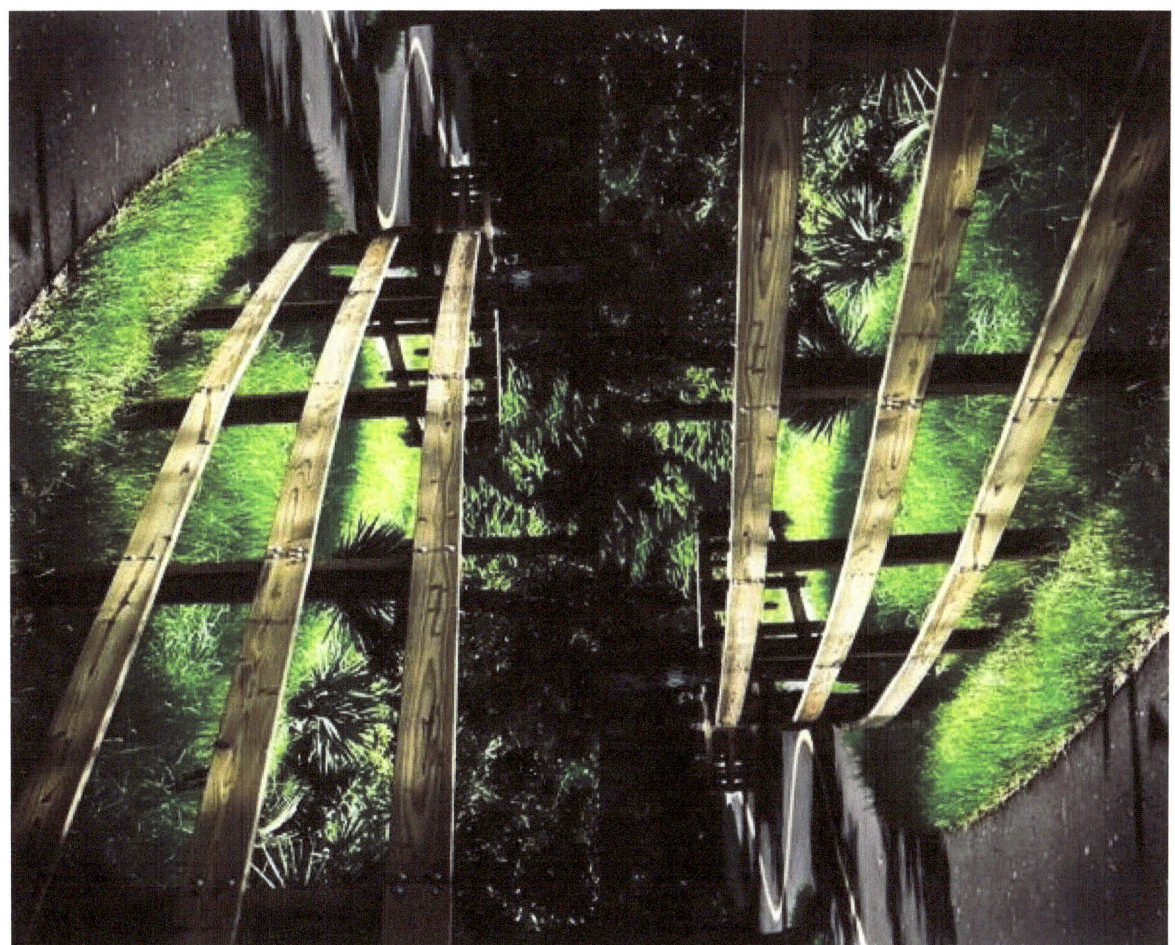

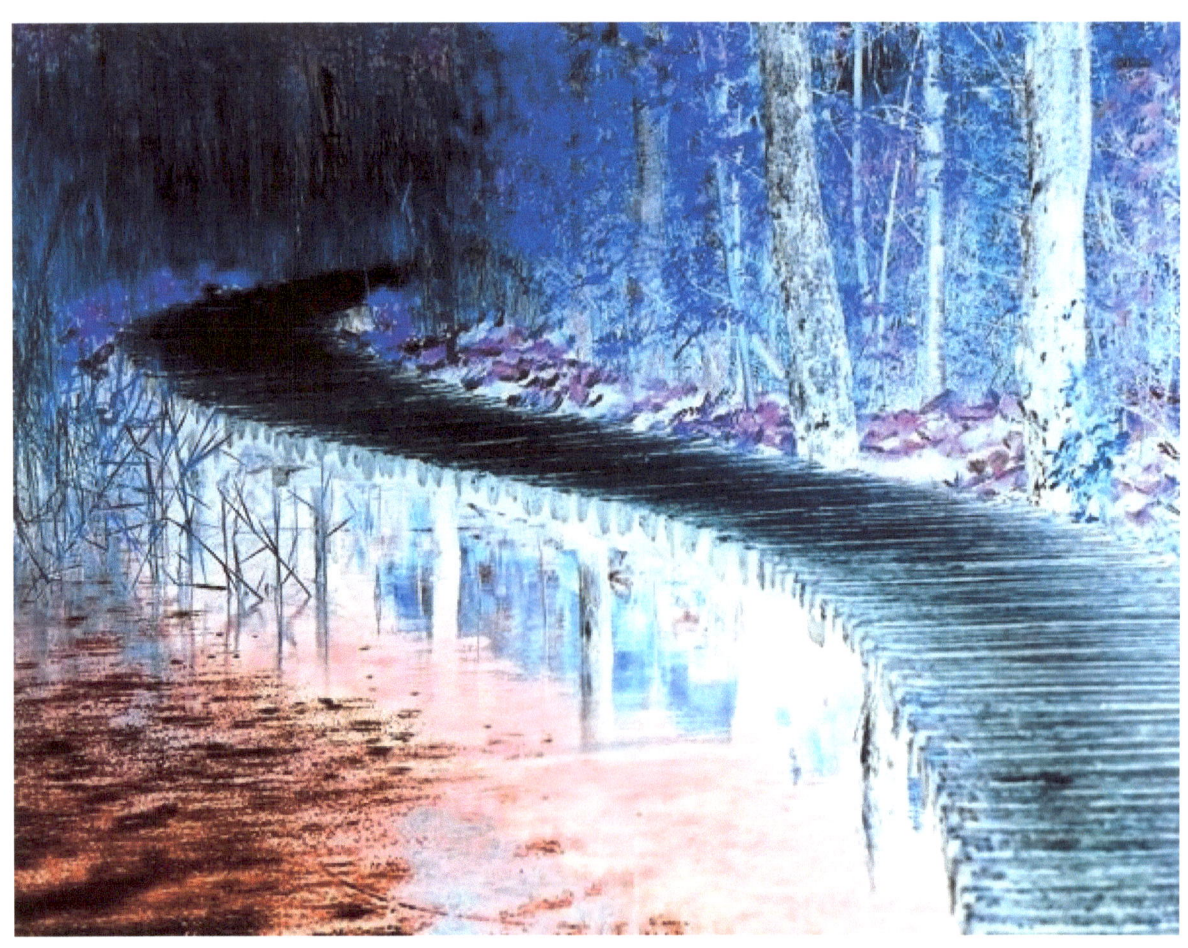
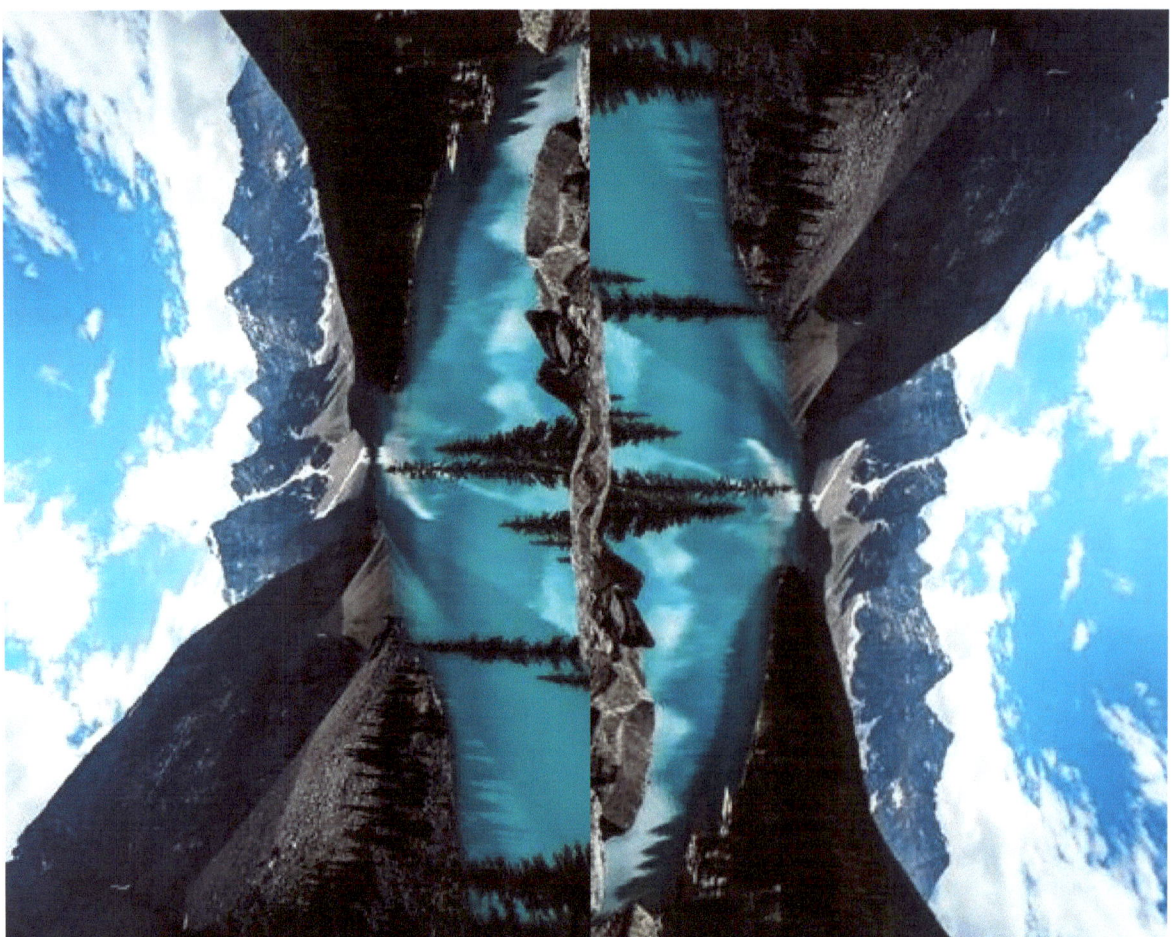

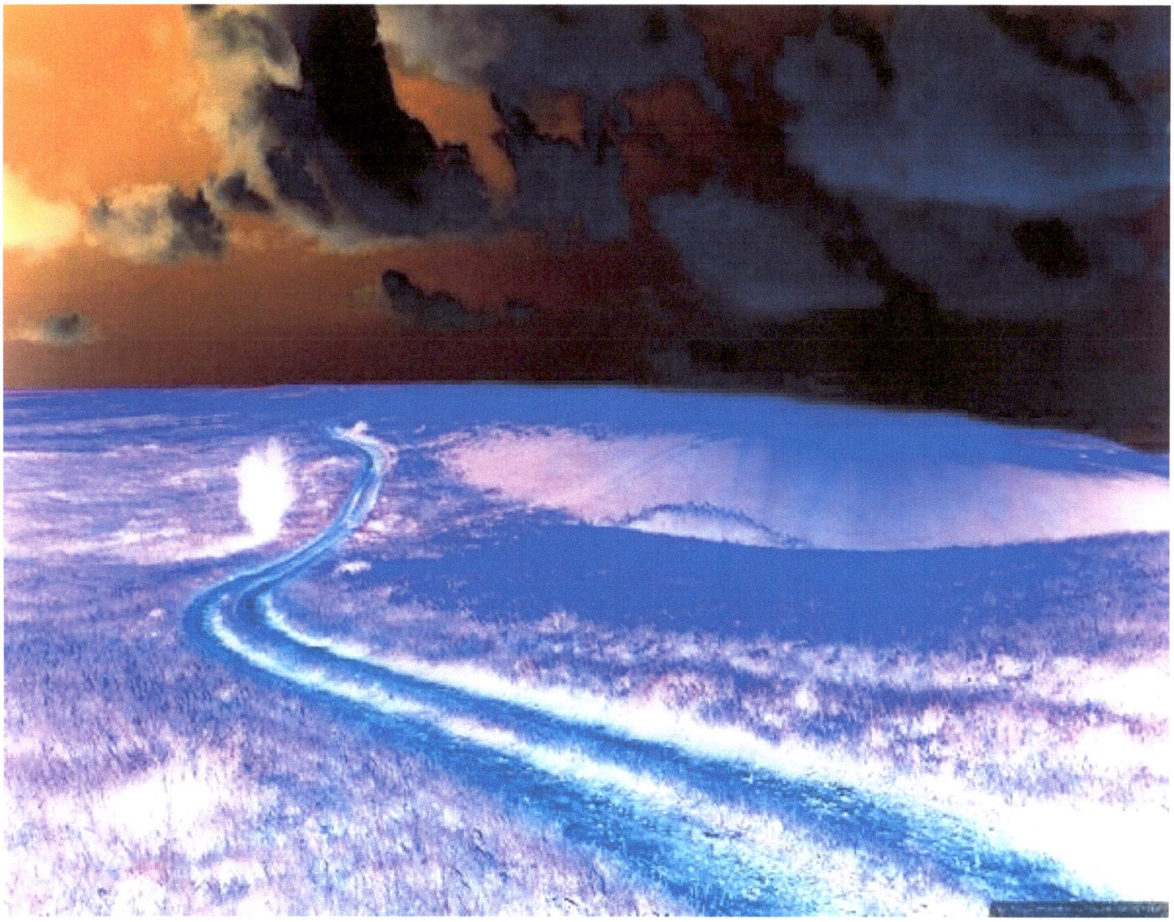

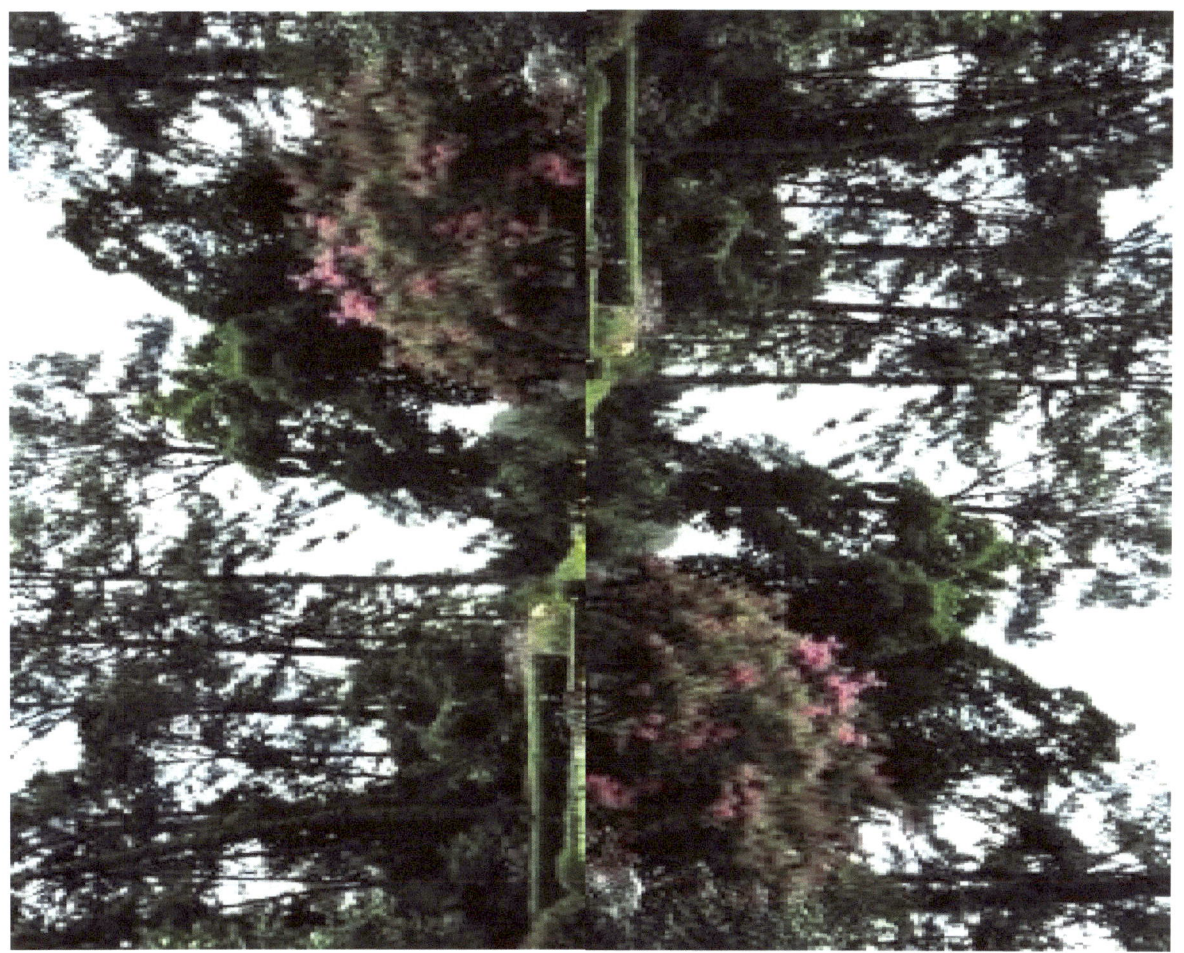

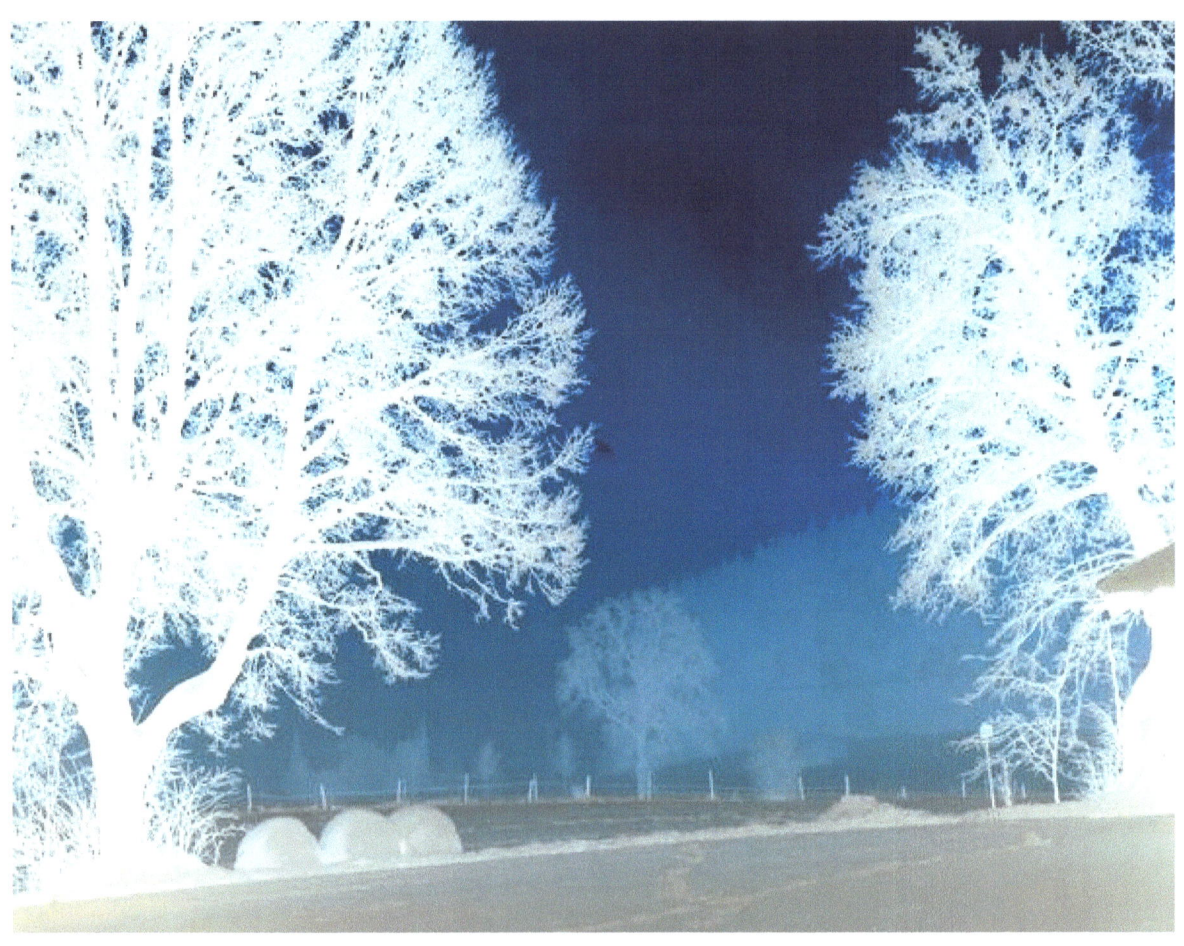
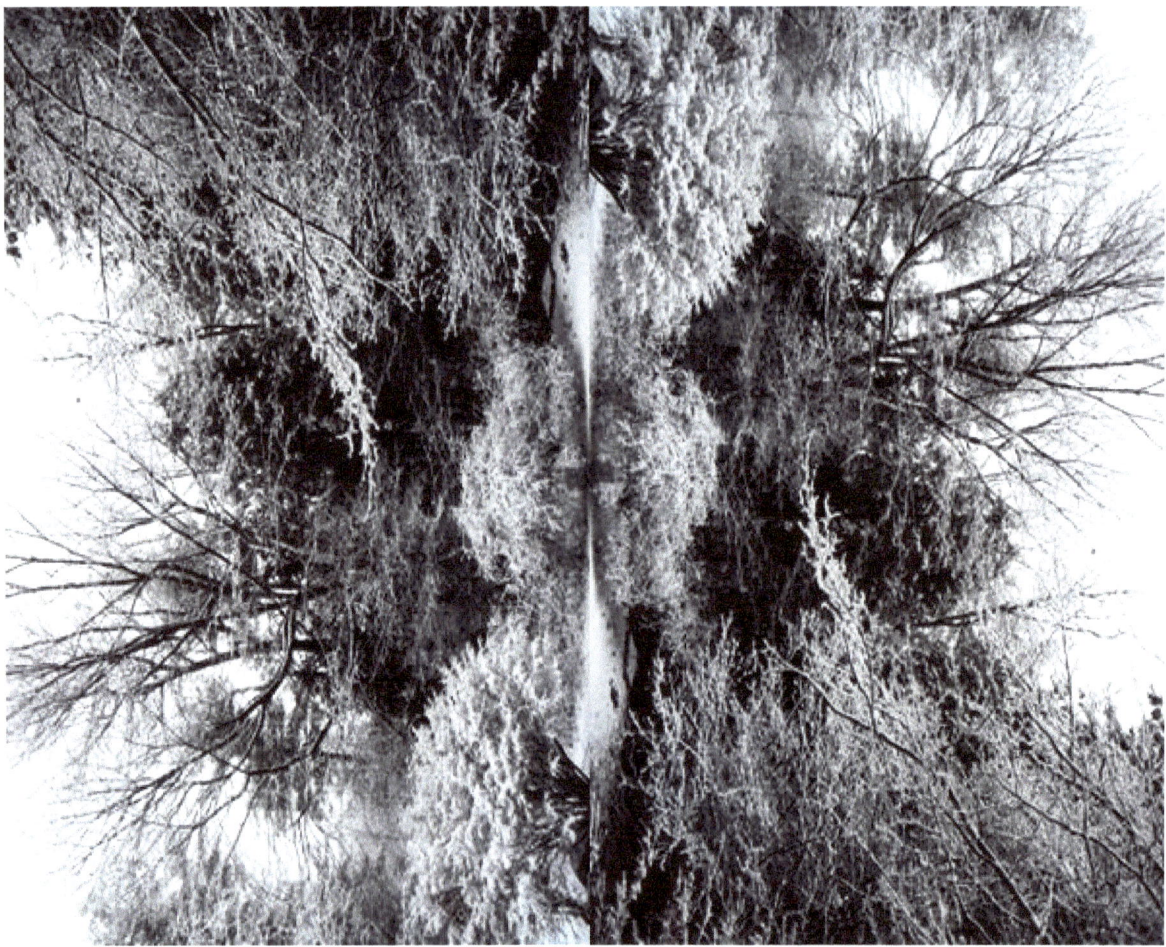

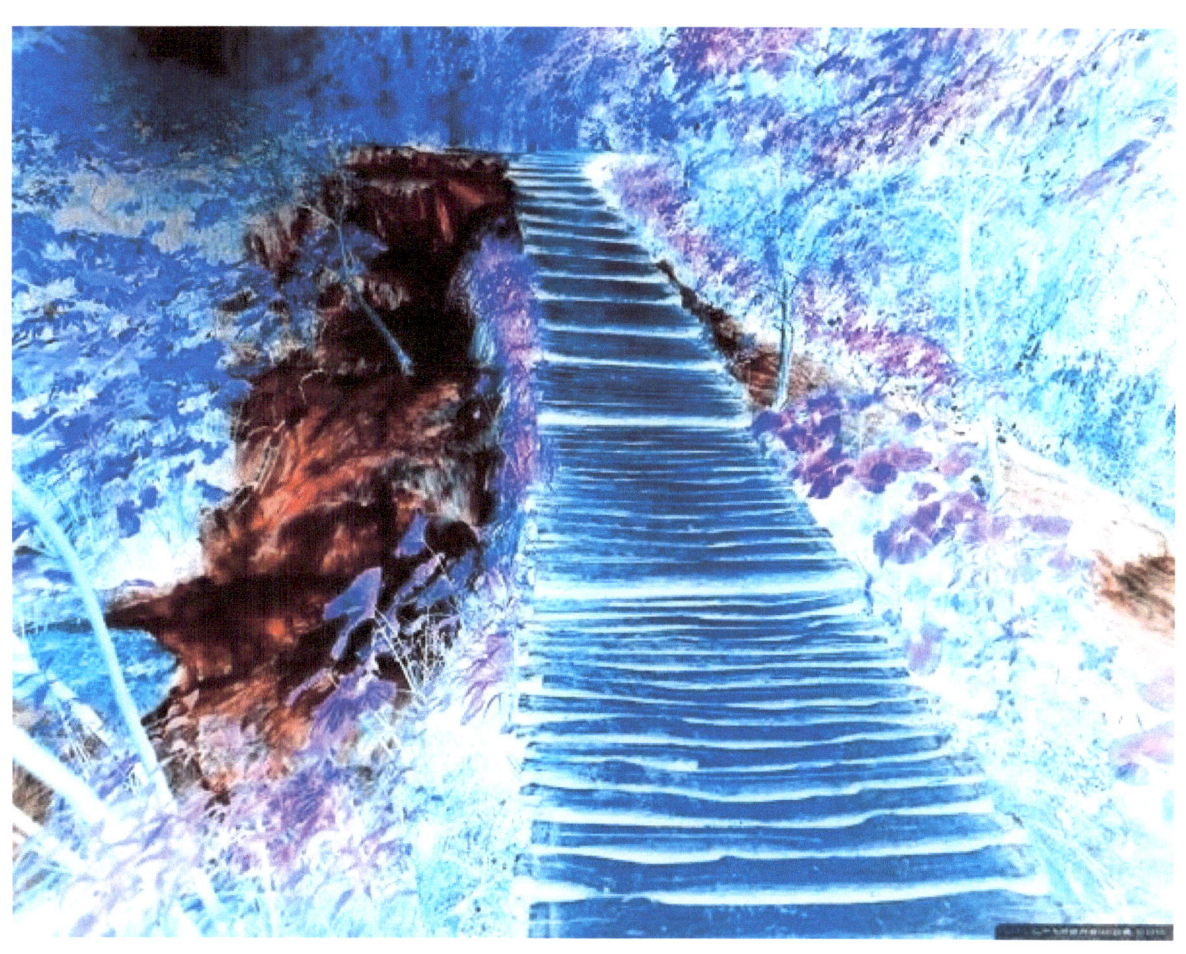
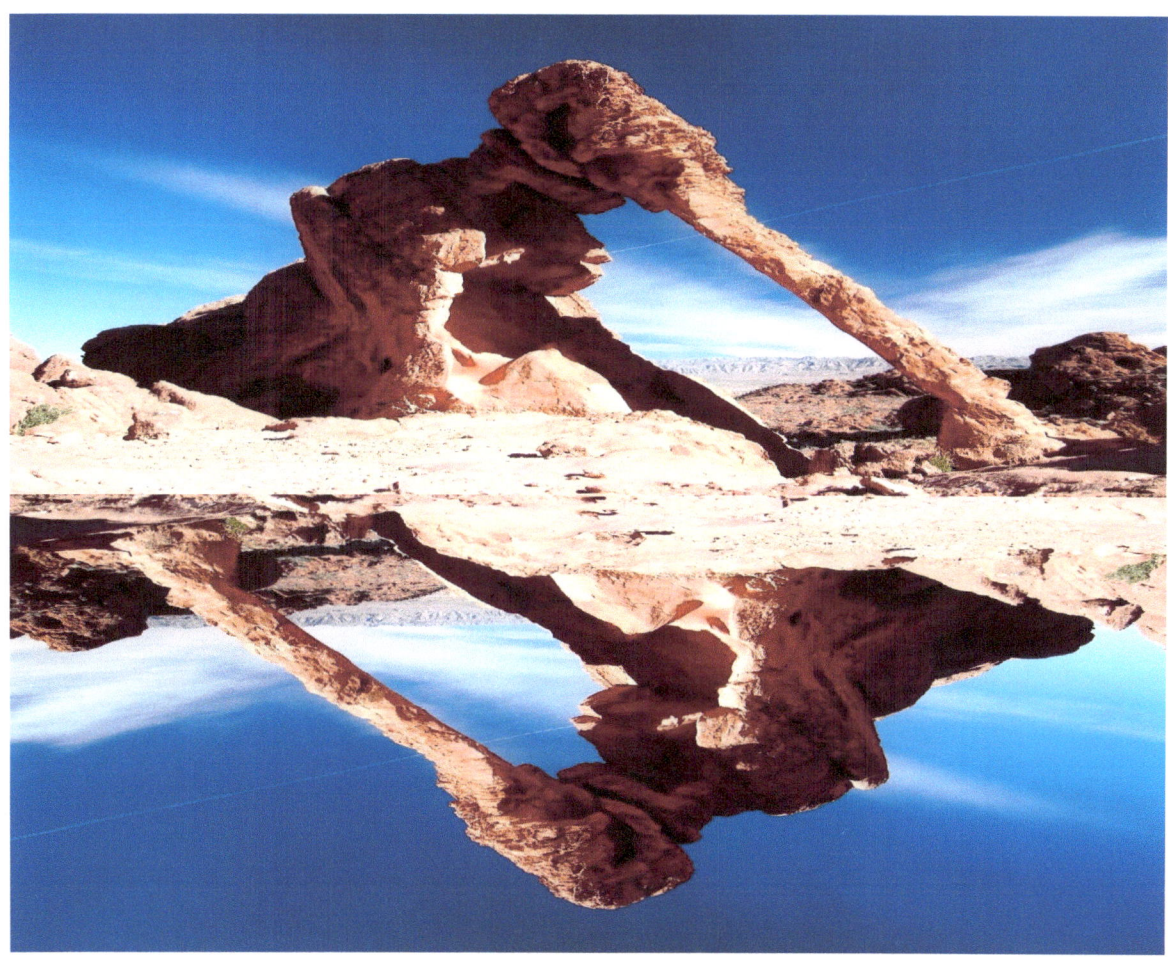

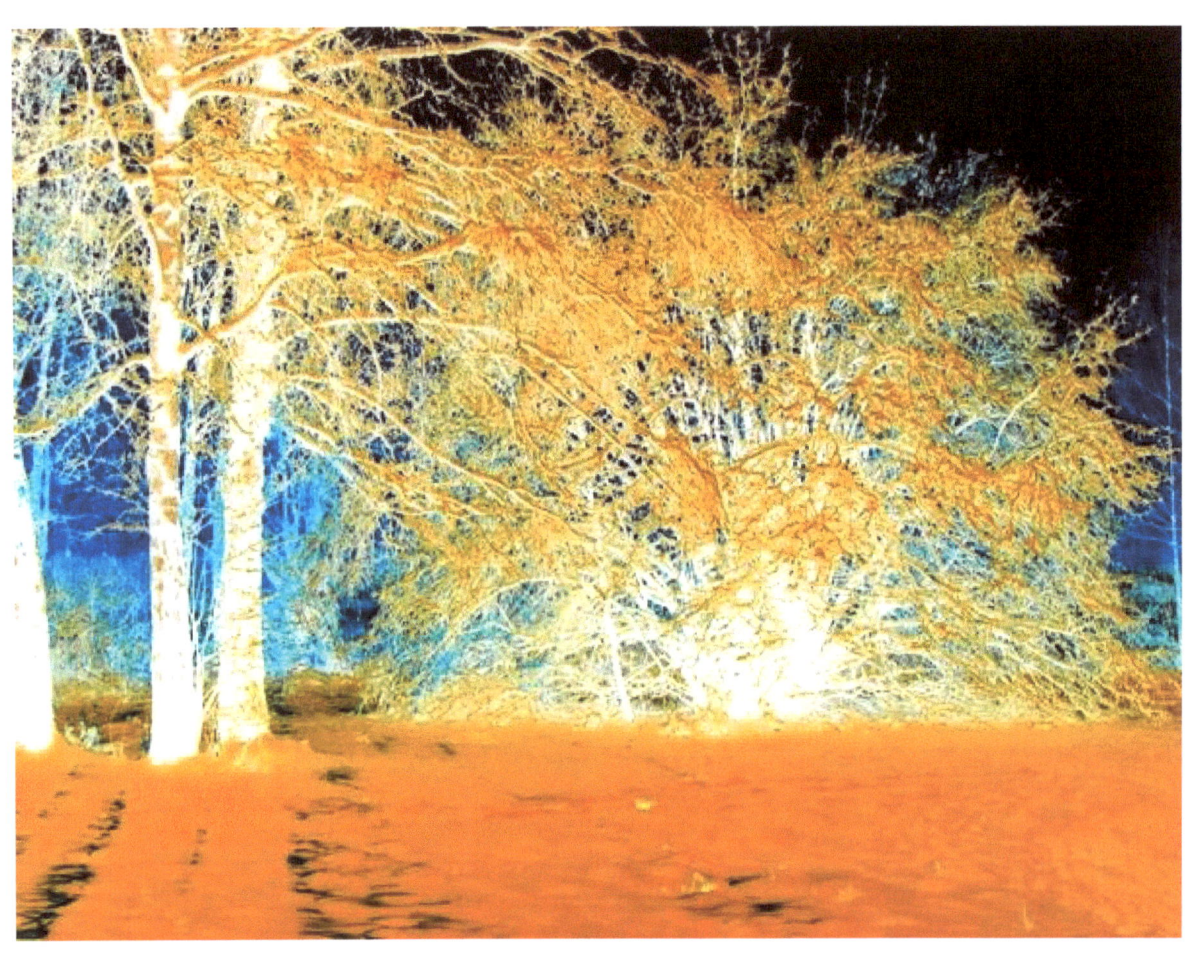
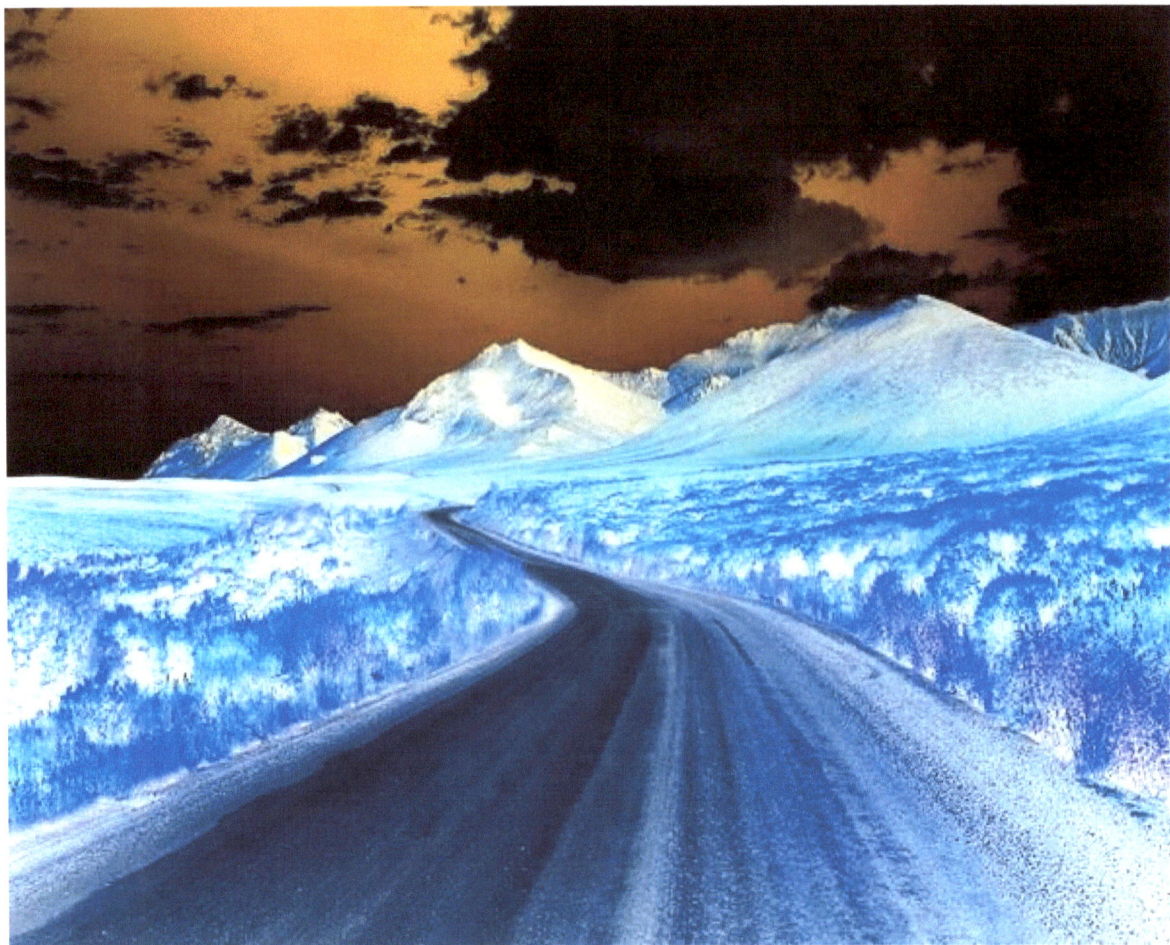

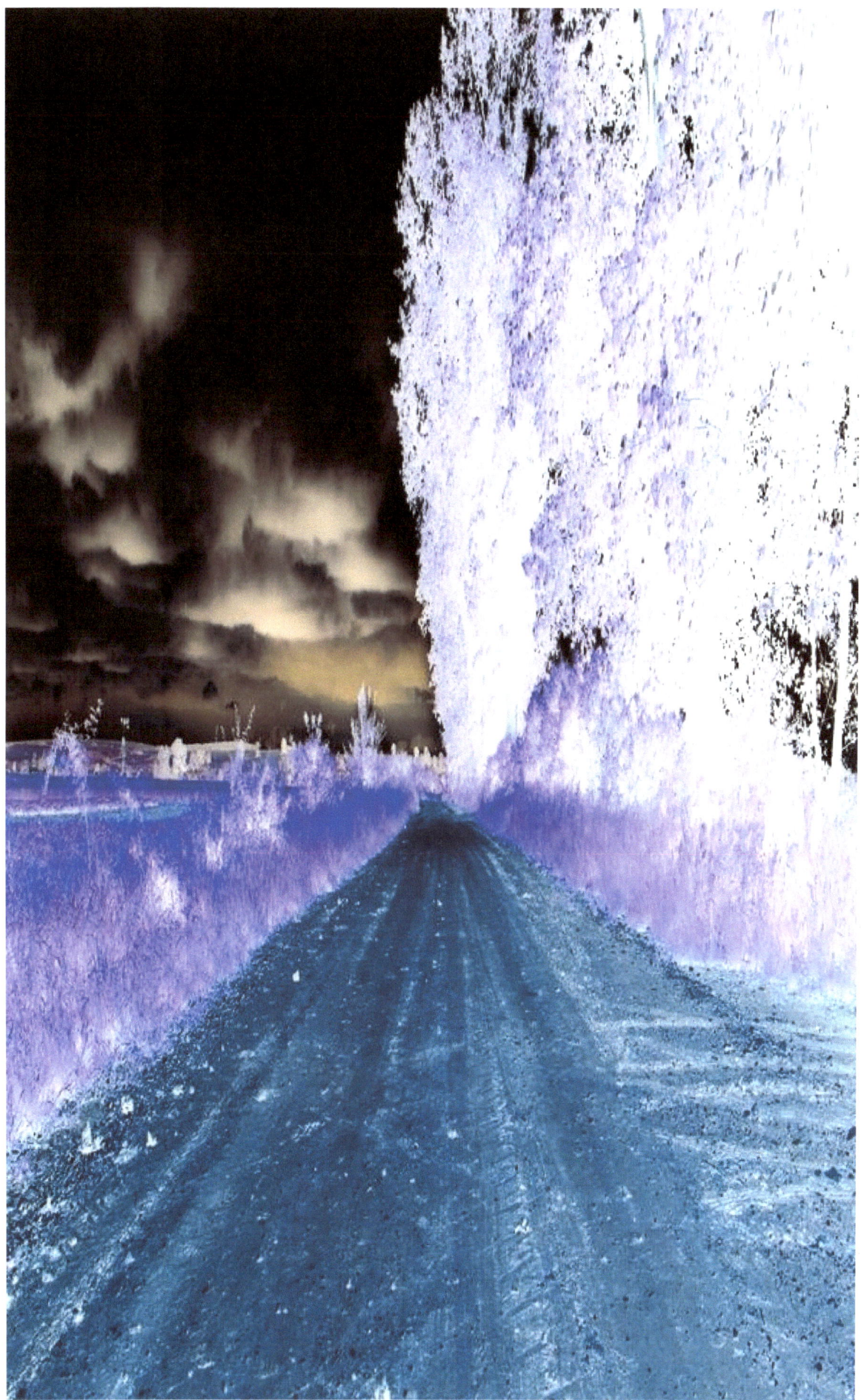

Beautiful Inverted Nature
Arya Bàhram

www.ingramcontent.com/pod-product-compliance
Lightning Source LLC
Chambersburg PA
CBHW051826210526
45473CB00005B/1759